Shakespeare's Figures of Speech

By the same author

Non fiction

Shakespeare's Friends

Shakespeare's Family

Plays and Muicals for Adults

Rake and Moon Feasting

Dominion

Hats, Hats Off!

A Thousand Francs Reward

The Man Who Corrupted Hadleyberg

The Gift of the Magi

Inn Bethlehem

Columbus

Books for Children

Bravest of All

Fritzie Goes Home

Plays and Musicals for Children

The Shoemaker and the Christmas Elves

Freedom Train

The Firebird

Snow White and Rose Red

Sleeping Beauty

Operas for Children

The Starbird

St. George and the Dragon

Daniel and the Dream Catcher

The Adventures of Young Peer Gynt

Cinderella in Spain

The Velveteen Rabbit

Operas for Adults

The Impresario

Hadleyburg

The Masque of Evil

Shakespeare's Figures of Speech

A Reader's Guide

Kate Emery Pogue

iUniverse, Inc.
New York Bloomington

Shakespeare's Figures of Speech
A Reader's Guide

iUniverse books may be ordered through booksellers or by contacting:

iUniverse
1663 Liberty Drive
Bloomington, IN 47403
www.iuniverse.com
1-800-Authors (1-800-288-4677)

ISBN: 978-1-4401-5191-0 (pbk)
ISBN: 978-1-4401-5192-7 (ebk)

Printed in the United States of America

iUniverse rev. date: 7/9/2009

For Chesley and Elva
in gratitude for their faith in my work.

Acknowledgements

I am very grateful to my colleagues and friends who have been patient, helpful and sometimes even enthusiastic as I worked on this arcane material. I especially want to thank Drs. Ann Christensen, and Sidney Berger from the University of Houston; Drs Merrilee Cunningham, Susan Baker, Susan Ahern, Michael Dressman, Jean DeWitt, and Thomas J. Lyttle from the University of Houston Downtown; Drs. James Shapiro, Tiffany Stern, and the Rice Fondren and Folger Shakespeare Libraries. I give a special thank-you to Jerilyn Watson for housing me in Washington, D.C; to my Shakespeare Class at the West University Senior Center; to James Dick and the International Festival Institute at Round Top, Texas; and to my husband Bill for his keen editorial eye and his patience in combing through the manuscript searching out my errors.

Contents

Preface

There are many books about rhetoric and grammar, but none that narrows the topic to the specific area covered in this book: Shakespeare's usage of named figures of speech. Learning is based on the perception of pattern; without their names and definitions patterns are only half-perceived. In recognizing by name the patterns Shakespeare chose to structure his language we enhance our ability to appreciate his work. Therefore, for as long as we consider Shakespeare worth studying, this subject is and will be of crucial importance.

No modern reader can be expected to know all the terms and the patterns contained here; therefore this book is for the reader who recognizes that there are patterns in Shakespeare's writing and wants a resource to explain what they are called and of what they consist. *Shakespeare's Figures of Speech* is a dictionary or lexicon to help readers in their search for his patterns. Two sections list in alphabetical order the names of figures of speech: first (in Part I) the commonly known figures with definitions and examples; then (in Part II) the names and definitions of more arcane figures.

If the reader is trying to identify a device he or she has spotted, the Glossary lists the devices by types: Addition, Subtraction and Substitution of Letters and Syllables, for instance, or Amplification devices, or Repetitions. This will enable readers to trace devices they have observed back to the alphabetical listing in the main text, and thereby to the definition and examples.

The study of rhetorical and grammatical terms in Shakespeare's day is complex and often confusing. The researcher finds subtly different definitions of terms, or even more frequently two or more terms (sometimes one based on Latin another on Greek) meaning the same thing. What we now call rhetoric (in one of its many contemporary definitions) the Elizabethans called grammar, and they distinguished rhetorical structures (which also had classical names) from grammatical structures. There were a number of text books in Shakespeare's day and even they did not always agree on terminology and definitions.

In order to simplify the presentation in this book, when I discovered a confusing number of names in modern books seeming to describe the same thing I went back to the books of Shakespeare's day to find the terms as he would have learned them. One of the books I consulted was William Lily's *A Short Introduction of Grammar Generallie to be Used* (1557). Lily's Grammar was one of the pervasive texts of the time and one that Shakespeare himself probably used in school. In addition I relied on Richard A. Sherry's *A Treatise of Schemes & Tropes* (1550), and George Puttenham's *The Arte of English Poesie* (1589). Shakespeare would have left school by 1580 and so would not have known this latter book as a schoolboy. But I was struck by the charming way Puttenham assigned English terms to Latin or Greek names for figures. For instance he called the figure of Irony the Drie Mock; he called Paradox, the Wondrer; Anthimeria or Enallage, (the substitution of one part of speech – case, gender, person, tense, etc. – for another) the Changeling; and Emphasis, the Reinforcer. Puttenham, like an impressive number of educators of the time, was trying to make learning easier, more accessible, and more exciting for boys confined in a schoolroom studying grammar from six or seven in the morning until sun down. I found Puttenham's terms so delightful that I included as many as possible in my definitions. The fact that I have some definitions not included in Puttenham's list, but contained in Lily, say, or Sherry, illustrates how complicated this subject is.

The listing of figures of speech in this book is representative, not comprehensive. There are easily twice the number of figures I've chosen here. For the reader eager to go into a deeper study of Shakespeare's rhetoric, the most important twentieth century works are those of Sister Miriam Joseph: *Shakespeare's Use of the Arts of Language* (reprinted by Paul Dry Books, 2005) and *The Trivium* (Paul Dry Books, 2002). I also found of great use George T. Wright's *Shakespeare's Metrical Art*; (University of California Press, 1988) and Richard A. Lanham's *A Handlist of Rhetorical Terms* (University of California Press, 1968). All the above books are more vast than this one in scope, addressing the entire complicated subject of early modern rhetoric and grammar.

For those desiring to know how Shakespeare's figures of speech affect stage direction and performance, I recommend the excellent book by Leslie O'Dell called *Shakespearean Language, A Guide for Actors and Students*. (Praeger, 2002). Written with actors in mind, her insights are valuable to any Shakespearean devotee, and her treatment of the patterns of language in the chapter entitled "Acquiring an Elizabethan Rhetorical Facility" is comprehensive and masterful.

In *Shakespeare's Figures of Speech* I have constricted the focus. I simply want to set out clearly names and examples of most of the linguistic devices that Shakespeare used, and to help the reader apprehend how they shape the content of his work.

KEY TO REFERENCES

SUAL	*Shakespeare's Use of the Arts of Language.* Sister Miriam Joseph
TRI	*The Trivium.* Sister Miriam Joseph
HRT	*A Handlist of Rhetorical Terms.* Richard A. Lanham
SL	*Shakespearean Language.* Leslie O'Dell
SMA	*Shakespeare's Metrical Art.* George T. Wright
WS	*William Shakespeare, a Biography.* A.L. Rowse
WTWTW	*Where There's a Will There's a Way.* Leslie McGuire
Puttenham	*The Arte of English Poesie* [1589]. George Puttenham

Foreword

This book will change the way you read Shakespeare. It will also change your perception of how Shakespeare wrote his plays.

The twenty-first century reader looks at the language of Shakespeare for meaning, sonority, rhythm, and connotation; and after four hundred years of changes in the English language, achieving just this level of understanding is often a challenge.

However, Shakespeare gives the reader another key to his intention: his use of the verbal patterns called linguistic or literary figures of speech. When he was a child at school, Shakespeare was taught these patterns as crucial means of expression. Like every other schoolboy of his age, Shakespeare learned to name the figures, then practiced translating them from Latin into English, after which he and his schoolmates were challenged to recreate the figures in Latin and English writings of their own. So, for Shakespeare as an adult playwright, these patterns existed in his mind as learned and well-practiced usages.

When we read Shakespeare's plays with a knowledge of, and sensitivity to, his patterns of language, an entirely new level of emotion and meaning emerges: we perceive a heightened union of form and content without which we cannot experience the deepest aesthetic pleasure his great works offer.

Introduction

When William Shakespeare took up his pen to write his plays and poems, he brought to the task a mind filled with linguistic and structural devices, content radically different from that in the minds of twentieth and twenty-first century dramatists. As a child in the Stratford grammar school he, like every other educated boy of his day, was made to learn the language structures of classical literature. In studying plays (an important part of the curriculum) young William Shakespeare had to memorize epigrams, speeches, and scenes from the plays of Terence, Plautus, and Seneca. Furthermore he had to learn proper classical terminology to analyze play structures, and in addition to recognize between two and three hundred Latin tropes or figures of speech which patterned the language of those plays. To prove their knowledge of these many patterns, Shakespeare and the other boys were required to write in both English and Latin, using the devices they had memorized,

As an adult, Shakespeare drew on this highly patterned rhetoric, and used both the rhetorical structures and the linguistic devices consciously and unconsciously, instinctively and intellectually in his own writing. They were in his mind and at his fingertips when he picked up his quill; his stories, his images, his characters were shaped by their use.

A knowledge of Shakespeare's most commonly used rhetorical devices enhances our appreciation of his work, and an awareness of them is crucial to realizing how he went about writing. Manipulation of rhetorical devices is part of what gives Shakespeare's work its richness and depth. Tracing his development as a writer from the early plays to the late romances the reader sees the simplest, most easily recognizable, and most blatant use of named patterns in his early work. We appreciate, then, with a new awareness the increasing complexity of structure, subtlety of language, and individuality of writing style that emerges in his middle and later years.

For the actor and director of Shakespeare's plays, recognizing the rhetorical devices gives information on how a play builds and climaxes, the rhythms with which speeches should be spoken, where the actor is to breathe, what the phrasing should be, what words should be emphasized, and how a scene or speech is to be paced.

Today formal or classical rhetoric is not often taught, certainly not to the extent it was in Elizabethan times. This handbook hopes to fill an important gap in our ability to value Shakespeare's writing by presenting the name of each figure of speech or rhetorical device he used, with a clear definition of the device, followed by a variety of examples from Shakespeare's work.

Part 1: Familiar Rhetorical Terms

The figures of speech listed below in Part I are those still in common use today. Their names and usages are, or should be, familiar to the English reader of the twenty-first century.

Acrostic: **[Greek, from *akros*, extreme, and *stichos*, order, line, verse]**

A poem in which the first letter of each line, reading down, spells a hidden word or message. The first letters of the lines below, spoken by the Queen of the Fairies, spell out her name, Titania. Shakespeare used this device rarely as he was less interested in intellectual verbal conceits than in the use of figures to intensify emotion or to establish character.

Titania:
Thou shalt remain here, whether thou wilt or no,
I am a spirit of no common rate
The summer still doth tend upon my state;
And I do love thee. Therefore go with me.
I'll give thee fairies to attend on thee
And they shall fetch thee jewels from the deep…
(A *Midsummer Night's Dream*
Act III Scene 1)

Though not technically an acrostic, Shakespeare enjoys playing with the letters of Miranda's name in this speech of Ferdinand's:

Ferdinand:
<u>Admired Miranda!</u>
Indeed the top of <u>admiration</u>, worth
What's dearest to the world!
(The Tempest
Act III Scene 1)

In *Richard III* Richard (Gloucester) refers to a verbal puzzle, possibly an acrostic, used to condemn George Clarence to his death in the tower. Though Shakespeare does not give us the whole puzzle, this passage indicates their prevalence in the language-play of the time.

Gloucester:
This day should Clarence closely be mewed up,
About a prophecy, which says that G
Of Edward's heirs the murderer shall be. . . .
But what's the matter, Clarence? May I know?

Clarence:
Yea, Richard, when I know; for I protest
As yet I do not: but as I can learn,
He harkens after prophecies and dreams;
<u>And from the cross-row plucks the letter G,</u>
And says a wizard told him that by G
His issue disinherited should be;
And for my name of George begins with G,
It follows in his thoughts that I am he.
(Richard III
Act I Scene 1)

Adage: **[Latin, *adagium, adagio,* I say]**

A brief proverb or familiar saying. See **Apothegm** in **<u>Part II</u>** below.

The use of an **adage** rather than original speech constructions indicates a conventional, pompous, shallow, or naive mentality and therefore is a Shakespearean characterization device.

Polonius:
<u>Neither a borrower nor a lender be</u>. . .
<u>To thine own self be true</u>. . .
(Hamlet
Act I Scene 3)

Lysander:
<u>The course of true love never did run smooth</u>.
(A Midsummer Night's Dream
Act I Scene 1)

Caesar:
<u>Cowards dies many times before their deaths;</u>
<u>The valiant never taste of death but once</u>.
(Julius Caesar
Act II Scene 2)

Lady Macbeth disparages her husband's vacillations using the term **adage,** one of the many references to linguistic devices that reveal Shakespeare's consciousness of the patterns he was using.

Lady Macbeth:
Wouldst thou have that
Which thou esteem'st the ornament of life,
And live a coward in thine own esteem,
Letting 'I dare not' wait upon 'I would',
<u>Like the poor cat I'th'adage</u>?
(Macbeth
Act I Scene 6)

Alliteration: **[Latin, *ad*, to and *littera*, letter]**

The repetition of two or more words beginning with the same sound.

I perceive that men as plants increase,
Cheered and checked even by the selfsame sky.,
(Sonnet #15)

Bottom:
For by thy gracious, golden, glittering gleams
I trust to taste of truest Thisbe sight.
(A Midsummer Night's Dream Act V Scene 1)

King Henry:
I see you stand like greyhounds in the slips,
Straining upon the start. The game's afoot:
Follow your spirit. . . .
(Henry V Act III Scene 1)

Ambiguity: **[Latin, *ambiguus,* doubtful]**

Using words to mean two or more things at once. The richness of characterization and thought in Shakespeare's plays can often be traced to his subtle use of **ambiguity**. For a related figure see **Irony**.

Gloucester:
Bring me but to the very brim of it,
And I'll repair the misery thou dost bear
With something rich about me: from that place

I shall no leading need.
(King Lear
Act IV Scene 1)

Leontes:
Hermione, my dearest, thou never spok'st
To better purpose.
(The Winter's Tale
Act I Scene 2)

Decius:
Caesar, all hail! Good morrow, worthy
Caesar;
I come to fetch you to the Senate House.
(Julius Caesar
Act II Scene 2)

Amplification: [Latin, from *amplificore*, to make large]

Adding explanatory details to develop an idea, thought, or image.

Queen Margaret:
Great lords, wise men ne'er sit and wail their
loss,
But cheerly seek how to redress their harms.
What though the mast be now blown
overboard,
The cable broke, the holding-anchor lost,
And half our sailors swallowed in the flood?
Yet lives our pilot still. Is't meet that he
Should leave the helm, and like a fearful lad
With tearful eyes add water to the sea,
And give more strength to that which hath too
much,
Whiles, in his moan, the ship splits on the
rock,

Which industry and courage might have
saved?
Ah, what a shame! Ah, what a fault were this!
Say Warwick was our anchor; what of that?
And Montague our topmast; what of him?
Our slaughtered friends the tackles; what of
these?
Why, is not Oxford here another anchor?
And Somerset another goodly mast?
The friends of France our shrouds and
tacklings?
And though unskilful, why not Ned and I
For once allowed the skilful pilot's charge?
We will not from the helm to sit and weep,
But keep our course, though rough and wind
say no,
From shelves and rocks that threaten us with
wrack.
As good to chide the waves as speak them
fair.
And what is Edward but a ruthless sea?
What Clarence but a quicksand of deceit?
And Richard but a ragged fatal rock?
All these the enemies to our poor bark.
Say you can swim; alas, 'tis but a while!
Tread on the sand' why, there you quickly
sink:
Bestride the rock; the tide will wash you off,
Or else you famish; that's a threefold death.
This speak I, lords, to let you understand,
If case some one of you would fly from us,
That there's no mercy with the brothers
More than with ruthless waves, with sands
and rocks.
Why, courage then! What cannot be avoided
'Twere childish weakness to lament or fear.
(Henry VI Part 3
Act V Scene 4)

Titania:
. . . with thy brawls thou has disturb'd our sport.
Therefore the winds, piping to us in vain,
As in revenge have suck'd up from the sea
Contagious fogs; which, falling in the land,
Hath every pelting river made so proud
That they have overborne their continents.
The ox hath therefore stretch'd his yoke in vain,
The ploughman lost his sweat, and the green corn
Hath rotted ere his youth attain'd a beard;
The fold stands empty in the drowned field,
And crows are fatted with the murrion flock;
The nine-men's-morris is fill'd up with mud,
And the quaint mazes in the wonton green
For lack of tread are undistinguishable.
The human mortals want their winter cheer:
No night is now with hymn or carol blest.
Therefore the moon, the governess of floods,
Pale in her anger, washes all the air,
That rheumatic diseases do abound.
And thorough this distemperature we see
The seasons alter: hoary-headed frosts
Fall in the fresh lap of the crimson rose;
And on old Hiems' thin and icy crown,
An odorous chaplet of sweet summer buds
Is, as in mockery, set; the spring, the summer,
The childing autumn, angry winter, change
Their wonted liveries; and the 'mazed world,
By their increase, now knows not which is which.

(A Midsummer Night's Dream
Act II Scene 1)

Analogy: **[Greek, from *analogas*, analogous]**

A partial likeness between two things that are compared; for related figures see **Simile** and **Metaphor**.

Shall I compare thee to a summer's day?
Thou art more lovely and more temperate:
Rough winds do shake the darling buds of May,
And summer's lease hath all too short a date:
Sometime too hot the eye of heaven shines,
And often is his gold complexion dimm'd,
And every fair from fair sometime declines,
By chance, or nature's changing course untrimm'd:
But thy eternal summer shall not fade,
Nor lose possession of that fair thou ow'st,
Nor shall death brag thou wander'st in his shade,
When in eternal lines to time thou grow'st,
So long as men can breathe, or eyes can see,
So long lives this, and this gives life to thee.
(Sonnet #18)

Gloucester:
Look, how this ring encompasseth my finger.
Even so thy breast encloseth my poor heart;
Wear both of them, for both of them are thine.
(Richard III
Act I Scene 2)

Hippolyta:
Four days will quickly steep themselves in night.
Four nights will quickly dream away the time:

And then the moon, like to a silver bow
New-bent in heaven, shall behold the night
Of our solemnities.
(A Midsummer Night's Dream
Act I Scene 1)

Anecdote: **[Greek, *anekdotas*, things unpublished, *an*, priv. and *ekdotos*, published]**

The telling of an interesting event or episode. This rhetorical technique enlivens dialogue and illuminates situation and character by implying an **analogy** between the **anecdote** and the present circumstance.

Puck:
The king doth keep his revels here tonight;
Take heed the queen come not within his sight;
For Oberon is passing fell and wrath
Because that she as her attendant hath
A lovely boy, stol'n from an Indian king –
She never had so sweet a changeling;
And jealous Oberon would have the child
Knight of his train, to trace the forests wild:
But she perforce withholds the loved boy,
Crowns him with flowers and makes him all her joy.
(A Midsummer Night's Dream
Act II Scene 1)

Cassius:
I was born as free as Caesar, so were you;
We both have fed as well, and we can both
Endure the winter's cold as well as he.
For once, upon a raw and gusty day,
The troubled Tiber chafing with her shores,

Caesar said to me 'Dar'st thou, Cassius, now
Leap in with me into this angry flood,
And swim to yonder point?' Upon my word,
Accoutred as I was, I plunged in
And bade him follow: so indeed he did.
The torrent roared, and we did buffet it
With lusty sinews, throwing it aside
And stemming it with hearts of controversy.
But ere we could arrive the point proposed,
Caesar cried 'Help me, Cassius, or I sink!'
I, as Aeneas our great ancestor
Did from the flames of Troy upon his shoulder
The old Anchises bear, so from the waves of Tiber
Did I the tired Caesar: and this man
Is now become a god, and Cassius is
A wretched creature, and must bend his body
If Caesar carelessly but nod on him.
(Julius Caesar
Act I Scene 2)

Titania:
Set your heart at rest,
The fairy land buys not the child of me.
His mother was a vot'ress of my order;
And in the spiced Indian air, by night,
Full often hath she gossiped by my side;
And sat with me on Neptune's yellow sands,
Marking the embarked traders on the flood;
When we have laughed to see the sails conceive
And grow big-bellied with the wanton wind;
Which she, with pretty and with swimming gait
Following – her womb then rich with my young squire –

Would imitate, and sail upon the land,
To fetch me trifles, and return again,
As from a voyage, rich with merchandise.
But she, being mortal, of that boy did die;
And for her sake do I rear up the boy;
And for her sake I will not part with him.
(A Midsummer Night's Dream
Act II Scene 1)

Antithesis: **[Greek, *anti,* against and *tithenai,* to place or set]**

Setting one idea against another in opposition or contrast. This is a basic structure of Shakespearean language. Performers of Shakespeare will help audiences hear the structure of the language and its meaning by stressing (emphasizing) the nouns, verbs, adverbs, and adjectives that are antithetical to each other.

Brutus:
Let us be sacrificers, but not butchers,
Caius...
Let's kill him boldly, but not wrathfully.
(Julius Caesar
Act II Scene 1)

Helena:
The more my prayer, the lesser is my grace.
(A Midsummer Night's Dream
Act II Scene 2)

Puck:
Their sense thus weak, lost with their fears
thus strong.
(A Midsummer Night's Dream
Act III Scene 2)

Aphorism: **[Greek, *aphorismos*, a definition; a short, pithy sentence]**

Like **Adage** and **Apothegm** a pithy statement, or proverbial saying. When Shakespeare has characters speak often in **aphorisms** and **adages** he suggests a shallow-thinking, conservative individual, content to take another's thought for his own.

Helena:
Things base and vile, holding no quantity,
Love can transpose to form and dignity.
(A Midsummer Night's Dream Act I Scene 1)

Lysander:
The course of true love never did run smooth.
(A Midsummer Night's Dream Act I Scene 1)

Aside: A speech made directly to the audience, to oneself, or to another character, making sure the other character(s) on-stage neither hear nor attend. Shakespeare often uses asides to involve the audience directly in the action.

Romeo:
Look how she leans her cheek upon her hand
Would I were a glove upon that hand
That I might touch that cheek.
(Romeo and Juliet Act II Scene 2)

Buckingham:
Curses never pass
The lips of those that breathe them in the air.

Queen Margaret:
I will not think but they ascend the sky,
And there awake God's gentle-sleeping peace.
[aside] O Buckingham, take heed of yonder dog!
Look when he fawns, he bites' and when he bites,
His venom tooth will rankle to the death. . .
(Richard III
Act I Scene 3)

Bassanio:
Thou gaudy gold,
Hard food for Midas, I will none of thee—
Nor none of thee, thou pale and common drudge
'Tween man and man: but thou, thou meager lead,
Which rather threatn'st than dost promise aught,
Thy plainness moves me more than eloquence,
And here choose I – joy be the consequence!

Portia [aside]
How all the other passions fleet to air,
As doubtful thoughts, and rash-embraced despair,
And shudd'ring fear and green-eyed jealousy!
O love, be moderate, allay thy ecstasy,
In measure rain thy joy, scant this excess—
I feel too much thy blessing, make it less,
For fear I surfeit!
(The Merchant of Venice
Act III Scene 2)

Assonance: **[Latin, *assonans,* from *assonare*, to sound]**

The repetition of similar or identical vowel sounds. **Assonance** gives a beauty to the language, musical but more subtle than perfect **rhyme.**

Hamlet:
. . .arrows of outrageous fortune
. . .to sleep perchance to dream
(Hamlet
Act III Scene 1)

And with old woes new wail my dear time's waste.
(Sonnet #30)

Blank Verse: **[*blank*, lacking certain elements, i.e. rhyme]**

Lines of unrhymed iambic pentameter (see **Iambic Pentameter).** This was the favorite verse structure for dramatists in the English Renaissance. First explored in the university tragedy *Gorboduc* by two law students, Thomas Norton and Thomas Sackville in 1560-61, other dramatists rapidly discovered its flexibility and range. As a verse form it could accommodate high poetry as well as conversational practicality and its rhythm was a natural match for the English language. For actors, the rhythm of the blank verse line aided them in memorizing the vast amount of language required at the time. The examples below show the use of a regular rhythm. Shakespeare enjoyed diversifying the strict rhythm, finding less regular lines gave more range for expression as they played against the expected regular beat.

Juliet:
<u>Thou knowst the mask of night is on my face;</u>
<u>Else would a maiden blush bepaint my cheek,</u>
<u>For that which thou hadst heard me speak</u>
<u>tonight.</u>
(Romeo and Juliet
Act II Scene 2)

King Henry:
<u>How yet resolves the governor of the town</u>?
<u>This is the latest parle we will admit</u>:
Therefore to our best mercy give yourselves,
Or like to men proud of destruction,
Defy us to our worst: for, as I am a soldier,
<u>A name that in my thoughts becomes me best,</u>
If I begin the battery once again
<u>I will not leave the half-achieved Harfleur</u>
Till in her ashes she lie buried.
(Henry V
Act III Scene 3)

In the quotation from *Hamlet* below the lines most frequently end with an extra light syllable (as does the fifth line in the quote above from *Henry V*). These eleven-syllable lines are called feminine-ended lines and are an acceptable variation of the strongly accented ten syllable masculine line. A feminine ending can suggest ambivalence or lack of resoluteness in the speaker.

Hamlet:
To be or not to be that is the <u>question</u>.
Whether is nobler in the mind to <u>suffer</u>
The slings and arrows of outrageous <u>fortune</u>
Or to take arms against a sea of <u>troubles</u>
And by opposing end them. To die, to sleep.
(Hamlet
Act III Scene 1)

Here is a **sonnet** where twelve of the fourteen lines have a feminine ending:

Farewell! Thou art too dear for my
possessing,
And like enough thou know'st thy estimate.
The charter of thy worth gives thee releasing:
My bonds in thee are all determinate.
For how do I hold thee but by thy granting,
And for that riches where is my deserving?
The cause of this fair gift in me is wanting,
And so my patent back again is swerving.
Thy self thou gav'st, thy own worth then now
knowing,
Or me to whom thou gav'st it, else mistaking.
So thy great gift upon misprision growing,
Comes home again, on better judgment
making.
Thus have I had thee as a dream doth
flatter,
In sleep, a king, but waking no such
matter.
(Sonnet #87)

Caesura: **[Latin, *caedere*, to cut]**

A break or pause in the middle of a poetic line. When a performer or reader acknowledges the caesura by a change of pitch, intonation, or the briefest of pauses, the meaning of the line becomes clearer.

Gloucester:
Now is the winter / of our discontent
Made glorious summer / by this sun of York.
(Richard III
Act I Scene 1)

Richard:
We are amazed, / and thus long have we stood
To watch the fearful bending/ of thy knee,
Because we thought ourself / thy lawful king:
And if we be / how dare thy joints forget
To pay their awful duty / to our presence?
(Richard II
Act III Scene 3)

Julia:
How many women / would do such message?
Alas, poor Proteus, / thou hast entertained
A fox / to be the shepherd of thy lambs;
Alas, poor fool, / why do I pity him
That with his very heart / despiseth me?
(The Two Gentlemen of Verona
Act IV Scene 4)

Classical allusions: The reference to classical myths, personages, places, to intensify a present circumstance; see **Analogy**. All education in Shakespeare's day was based on the classics, the Bible, and the English prayer book. Therefore Shakespeare knew his audience would catch his **allusions**.

Lucentio:
Hark, Tranio, thou may'st hear <u>Minerva</u> speak.
(The Taming of the Shrew
Act 1 Scene 1)

Hermia:
I swear to thee by <u>Cupid</u>'s strongest bow. . .
(A Midsummer Night's Dream
Act 1 Scene 1)

Helena:
Apollo flies, and Daphne holds the chase;
The dove pursues the griffin, the mild hind
Makes speed to catch the tiger.
(A Midsummer Night's Dream
Act II Scene 2)

Rosalind:
*I'll have no worse name than Jove's own **pa**ge,*
And therefore look you call me Ganymede.
(As You Like It
Act 1 Scene 3)

Consonance: **[Latin, *con*, with and *sonare,* to sound]**

Sometimes called off-rhymes, sour rhymes or (when applicable as in 'good' and 'blood') visual rhymes. The consonants rhyme perfectly, but the vowel sounds imperfectly. Consonance is very commonly found later in the poetry of Emily Dickinson. Note: what may seem **consonance** with today's pronunciation may have been perfect **rhyme** four hundred years ago. Words set out as rhymes are indicators to linguists of the progressive change in the pronunciation of a language.

Katharina:
Our strength as weak, our weakness past compare,
That seeming to be most which we indeed least are.
Then veil your stomachs, for it is no boot
And place your hands below your husband's foot. . .
(The Taming of the Shrew
Act V Scene 2)

Wishing me like to one more rich in hope
Featured like him, like him with friends
possessed ,
Desiring this man's art and that man's scope
With what I most enjoy contented least. . .
(Sonnet #29)

Couplet: **[French, a diminutive of *couple*, a couple]**

Two lines of verse that rhyme, used often by Shakespeare as a coda to end a beat, a scene, or an act. The ears of the Shakespearean audience were used to listening for these endings and to hear them as powerful structural devices. At times, particularly in his early plays, entire speeches are made up of rhymed couplets. See *A Comedy of Errors, The Taming of the Shrew, The Two Gentlemen of Verona, A MidsummerNight's Dream.* Note the examples of **epilogues** below where the **epilogue** to *A Midsummer Night's Dream* and to *Henry VIII* are written all in rhymed couplets.

Prince:
Bear hence this body, and attend our will.
Mercy but murders, pardoning those that kill.
(Romeo and Juliet
Act III Scene 1)

Duncan:
Nor more that thane of Cawdor shall deceive
Our bosom interest: go pronounce his present
death,
And with his former title greet Macbeth.

Ross:
I'll see it done.

Duncan:
What he hath lost, noble Macbeth hath won.
(Macbeth
Act I Scene 2)

Queen:
Gone she is
To death or to dishonour, and my end
Can make good use of either. She being down,
I have the placing of the British crown.
(Cymbeline
Act III Scene 5)

Elision: **[Latin, *elidere*, to strike off]**

Contracting two words or two syllables of a word into one by omitting the weak vowel sound between them. Shakespeare used this device constantly as it gave flexibility in creating the rhythm of lines. The device is also called **hypermonosyllable**, and **syncope**. It is used repeatedly to tighten up the definite article with a following noun beginning with a vowel: *th'orient*, *th'earth.* It can also refer to consonants omitted to change a two-syllable word into one: *ne'er* for never, *e'en* for even.

King:
Thus did I keep my person fresh and new,
My presence like a robe pontifical,
Ne'er seen but wond'red at, and so my state,
Seldom but sumptuous, showed like a feast. .

(Henry IV Part I
Act III Scene 2)

Lucius:

What's thy interest
In this sad wreck? <u>*How came't? Who is't?*</u>
(Cymbeline
Act IV Scene 2)

Scarus:

Yon ribald-rid nag of Egypt –
Whom leprosy <u>*o'ertake! – i'th'midst o' th' fight,*</u>
When vantage like a pair of twins appeared,
Both as the same, or rather ours the elder –
The breeze upon her, like a cow in June! –
Hoists sails and flies.
(Antony and Cleopatra
Act III Scene 10)

Epilogue: **[Greek, *epi,* upon and *legein*, to say, speak; *epilogus*, a conclusion]**

A speech following the last scene of a play, addressed directly to the audience. Eight of Shakespeare's thirty-seven plays contain **epilogues** identified as such: *A Midsummer Night's Dream, Henry IV Part II, Henry V, As You Like It, All's Well that Ends Well, The Tempest, Henry VIII* and *Pericles*. *Troilus and Cressida* and *Richard III* contain final speeches (by Pandarus and Richmond respectively) that, in addressing the audience towards the end, take on the characteristics of an **epilogue,** while *Loves' Labour's Lost* and *Twelfth Night* end in songs which take the place of an **epilogue**. The prose **epilogue** of Rosalind in *As You Like* it contrasts with the iambic pentameter **epilogue** of *Henry VIII* below. Both, have the same theme in the end, not unusual with **epilogues**: the response of men and women in the audience to the play and to each other. Puck's **epilogue** at the end of *A Midsummer Night's Dream* and Prospero's at the end of *The Tempest are* in **tetrameters,** a shortened, four-beat line, as distinguished from **pentameter,** the five beat line that dominates the play itself.

> *Rosalind:*
> *It is not the fashion to see the lady the epilogue: but it is no more unhandsome than to see the lord the prologue. If it be true that good wine needs no bush, 'tis true that a good play needs no epilogue: yet to good wine they do use good bushes; and good plays prove the better by the help of good epilogues. . . What a case am I in then, that am neither a good epilogue nor cannot insinuate with you in the behalf of a good play! I am not furnished like a beggar, therefore to beg will not become me: my way is to conjure you, and I'll begin with the women. I charge you, O women, for the love you bear to men, to like as much of this play as please you: and I charge you, O men, for the love you bear to women – as I perceive by your simpering, none of you hates them – that between you and the women the play may please. If I were a woman, I would kiss as many of you as had beards that pleased me, complexions that liked me, and breaths that I defied not: and, I am sure, as many as have good beards, or good faces, or sweet breaths, will, for my kind offer, when I make curtsy, bid me farewell.*
>
> *(As You Like It Epilogue)*

Epilogue: (speaker unidentified)
'Tis ten to one this play can never please
All that are here. Some come to take their
ease,
And sleep an act or two; but those, we fear,
We've frightened with our trumpets; so, 'tis
clear,
They'll say 'tis naught; others, to hear the city
Abused extremely, and to cry 'that's witty!'
Which we have not done neither; that, I fear,
All the expected good we're like to hear
For this play at this time, is only in
The merciful construction of good women;
For such a one we showed 'em. If they smile
And say 'twill do, I know, within a while
All the best men are ours; for 'tis ill hap
If they hold when their ladies bid 'em clap.
(Henry VIII
Epilogue)

Puck:
If we shadows have offended
Think but this, and all is mended,
That you have but slumbered here
While these visions did appear.
And this weak and idle theme
No more yielding but a dream.
Gentles, do not reprehend.
If you pardon, we will mend.
And, as I am an honest Puck,
If we have unearned luck
Now to 'scape the serpent's tongue,
We will make amends ere long:
Else the Puck a liar call.
So, good night unto you all.

Give me your hands, if we be friends:
And Robin shall restore amends.
(A Midsummer Night's Dream
Epilogue)

Prospero:
Now my charms are all o'erthrown,
And what strength I have's my own,
Which is most faint: now, 'tis true,
I must be here confined by you,
Or sent to Naples. Let me not,
Since I have my dukedom got,
And pardoned the deceiver, dwell
In this bare island, by your spell.
But release me from my bands,
With the help of your good hands:
Gentle breath of yours my sails
Must fill, or else my project fails,
Which was to please: Now I want
Spirits to enforce . . . art to enchant—
And my ending is despair,
Unless I be reliev'd by prayer,
Which pierces so, that it assaults
Mercy itself, and frees all faults. . . .
As you from crimes would pardoned be,
Let your indulgence seet me free.
(The Tempest
Epilogue)

Epithet: **[Greek, *epititheni,* to put on; *epi,* on, *tithenai,* to put]**

A descriptive word or brief phrase applied to a person. In modern times the term has come to have a purely negative connotation, but in Shakespeare's day an **epithet** could be positive as well.

York:
O tigress' heart wrapt in a woman's hide!
(Henry VI Part 3
Act 1 Scene 4)

Petruchio:
You lie, in faith, for you are called plain Kate,
And bonny Kate, and sometimes Kate the curst:
But Kate, the prettiest Kate in Christendom.
(The Taming of the Shrew
Act II Scene 1)

Achilles:
To him, Patroclus. Tell him I humbly desire the valiant Ajax to invite the most valorous Hector to come unarmed into my tent, and to procure safe-conduct for his person of the magnanimous and most illustrious six-or-seven-times-honored Captain general of the Grecian army, Agamemnon, et cetera. Do this.
(Troilus and Cressida
Act III Scene 3)

Equivocation: **[Latin, *aequivocari*, to have the same sound]**

The use of language deliberately to mislead or be ambiguous; using vague or intentionally evasive language. See also **Ambiguity** and **Irony**. **Equivocation** was known to be used by people arrested for religious reasons in the Elizabethan and Jacobean period in hopes of avoiding clear language that might convict them.

Porter:
Knock, knock, knock! Who's there, i'th'name of Beelzebub? Here's a farmer, that hanged himself on th'expectation of plenty: come in, time-server; have napkins enow about you, here you'll sweat for't. Knock, knock! Who's there, in th'other devil's name? Faith, here's an equivocator, that could swear in both the scales against either scale, who committed treason enough for God's sake, yet could not equivocate to heaven: O, come in, Equivocator.

(Macbeth
Act II Scene 3)

Richard:
Mark, silent king, the moral of this sport,
How soon my sorrow hath destroyed my face.

Bolingbroke:
The shadow of your sorrow hath destroyed
The shadow of thy face.

(Richard II
Act IV Scene 1)

Beatrice:
I pray you, is Signior Mountanto returned from the wars or no?

Messenger:
I know of none of that name, lady.

Hero:
My cousin means Signior Benedick of Padua.

Messenger:
O, he's returned, and as pleasant as ever he was. . . .
And a good soldier too, lady.

Beatrice:
And a good soldier to a lady, but what is he to a lord?

Messenger:
A lord to a lord, a man to a man – stuffed with all honorable virtues.

Beatrice:
It is so, indeed. He is no less than a stuffed man, but for the stuffing –
Well, we are all mortal.
(Much Ado About Nothing Act I Scene 1)

Faults in Speech:

Malaprops: **[French, *mal* wrongly, *apropos*, concerning, about]**

Using the wrong word.

Dogberry:
Call up the right Master Constable. We have here recovered the most dangerous piece of lechery that was ever known in the Commonwealth.
(Much Ado About Nothing Act III Scene 4)

Dogberry:
Is our whole dissembly appeared?
(Much Ado About Nothing Act IV Scene 2)

Pistol:
His heart is <u>fracted</u> and <u>corroborate</u>
(Henry V
Act 2 Scene 2l)

Mistress Quickly:
He's in <u>Arthur's bosom</u>, if ever man went to <u>Arthur's bosom</u>.
(Henry V
Act 2 Scene 2)

Armado:
---but, sweet heart, I do implore secrecy— that the king would have me present the princess (sweet chuck!) with some delightful <u>ostentation</u>, or show, or pageant, or antic, or firework.
(Love's Labour's Lost
Act V Scene 1)

Confusion: [Latin, *confundere,* to pour together]

Deliberately muddling a dialogue.

Hamlet:
Not where he eats, but where a' is eaten - a certain convocation of politic worms are e'en at him: your worm is your only emperor for diet, we fat all creatures else to fat us, and we fat ourselves for maggots. Your fat king and your lean beggar is but variable service, to dishes, but to one table -- that's the end.
(Hamlet
Act IV Scene 3)

Digression: [Lation, *digressio*, a parting, separating]

Turning the subject to another concern.

Polonius:
Madame, I swear I use no art at all.
That he is mad 'tis true, 'tis pity,
And pity 'tis 'tis true -- a foolish figure.
But farewell it, for I will use no art.
(Hamlet
Act II Scene 2)

Comic syllogism:

Setting up a false logical progression for comedic effect

Touchstone:
Then learn this of me -- to have is to have; for it is a figure in rhetoric that drink, being poured out of a cup into a glass, by filling the one doth empty the other; for all your writers do consent that ipse is he: now you are not ipse, for I am he.
(As You Like It
Act V Scene 1)

Heroic Couplet: **[Greek, *herioikos,* pertaining to a hero]**

Two lines of rhymed **iambic pentameter**.

But if the while I think on thee, dear friend,
All losses are restored and sorrows end.
(Sonnet #30)

King Richard:
Go, muster men: my counsel is my shield;
We must be brief when traitors brave the field.
(Richard III
Act IV Scene 3)

Hamlet:
I'll have grounds
More relative than this. The play's the thing
Wherein I'll catch the conscience of the king.
(Hamlet
Act II Scene 2)

Heroic Quatrain: Four-line, five-stress verse rhymed a-b-a-b; the main unit of a Shakespearean **sonnet.**

Romeo:
If I profane with my unworthiest hand
This holy shrine, the gentle sin is this
My lips, two blushing pilgrims stand
To smooth that rough touch with a tender kiss.
(*Romeo and Juliet*
Act 1 Scene 4)

That time of year thou may'st in me behold
When yellow leaves, or none, or few, do hang
Upon those boughs which shake against the cold—
Bare ruined choirs where late the sweet birds sang.
(Sonnet # 73)

King:
So sweet a kiss the golden sun gives not
To those fresh morning drops upon the rose,
As thy eye-beams, when their fresh rays have

smote
The night of dew that on my cheeks down
flows . . .
(Love's Labour's Lost
Act IV Scene 3)

Hyperbole: [Greek, *hyberballein*, to throw beyond or over]

Exaggeration for effect, not to be taken seriously.

Troilus:
I am weaker than a woman's tear
Tamer than sheep, fonder than ignorance.
(Troilus and Cressida
Act 1 Scene 1)

Petruchio:
Think you a little din can daunt mine ears?
Have I not in my time heard lions roar?
Have I not heard the sea, puffed up with
winds
Rage like an angry boar chafed with sweat?
Have I not heard great ordnance in the field
And heaven's artillery thunder in the skies?
Have I not in a pitched battle heard
Loud 'larums, neighing steeds, and trumpets
clang?
And do you tell me of a woman's tongue
That gives not half so great a blow to hear
As will a chest nut in a farmer's fire?
Tush, tush, fear boys with bugs.
(The Taming of the Shrew
Act 1 Scene 2)

Iambic Pentameter: [Greek, *iambos* a metrical foot of two syllables, the first unaccented, the second accented; and *penta,* five; and *meter* from

metron, measure]

'Iambic' refers to the rhythmic pattern of a word like 'ago' – a light stress followed by a heavy stress. **'Pentameter'** means five such units. **Iambic pentameter** is the basic line of Shakespearean verse: a ten-syllable line of alternating light and heavy stresses:

Lorenzo:
How sweet the moonlight sleeps upon this bank.

(Merchant of Venice
Act V Scene 1)

I all alone beweep my outcast state.
(Sonnet #29)

Dumaine:
This will I send, and something else more plain.
(Love's Labour's Lost
Act IV Scene 3)

Irony: **[Greek, *eironeia,* dissimulation]**

Saying the opposite of what is meant:

Leontes:
Go play, boy, play. Thy mother plays and I
Play too.
(The Winter's Tale
Act I Scene 2)

Perhaps the most famous use of **irony** in all

Shakespeare is found in Mark Antony's funeral oration for Caesar where Brutus's honor is undermined with the **irony** used by Marc Antony:

> *Antony:*
> *The noble Brutus*
> *Hath told you Caesar was ambitious:*
> *If it were so, it was a grievous fault,*
> *And grievously hath Caesar answered it. . . .*
> *Here, under leave of Brutus and the rest,*
> *(For Brutus is an honorable man;*
> *So are they all; all honorable men)*
> *Come I to speak in Caesar's funeral. . . .*
> *He was my friend, faithful and just to me:*
> *But Brutus says he was ambitious;*
> *And Brutus is an honorable man. . . .*
> *He hath brought many captives home to Rome,*
> *Whose ransoms did the general coffers fill:*
> *Did this in Caesar seem ambitious?*
> *When that the poor have cried, Caesar hath wept:*
> *Ambition should be made of sterner stuff:*
> *Yet Brutus says he was ambitious;*
> *And Brutus is an honorable man.*
> *(Julius Caesar*
> *Act III Scene 2)*

Metaphor: **[Greek, *metaphora,* a transferring to one word the sense of another, from *meta*, over, and *pherein*, to bear]**

A comparison where one says or implies that something is something else:

Helena:
<u>I am your spaniel</u> and, Demetrius,
The more you beat me, I will fawn on you.
(A Midsummer Night's Dream
Act II Scene 1)

Gloucester:
Now is the <u>winter of our discontent</u>
Made glorious summer by this son of York.
(Richard III
Act I Scene 1)

. . . <u>those boughs</u> which shake against the cold,
<u>Bare ruined choirs</u> where once the sweet birds sang.
(Sonnet #73)

Macbeth:
<u>Life's but a poor player</u> that struts and frets his hour
Upon the stage..
(Macbeth
Act V Scene 5)

Meter: **[Greek, *metron*, measure]**

The regular arrangement of stress or emphasis in a poetic line.

Stress: Alternation of heavy and light emphasis on syllables in words or on words in phrases.

Name of the meter

Example

2 Foot Meters	***iamb***	**- /**	***de<u>light</u>***
	trochee	**/ -**	***<u>sple</u>ndid***

	spondee	//	***bright-shod***
	phyrric	- -	***with a***
3 Foot Meters	***dactyl***	/ - -	***tenderly***
	amphibrach	- / -	***delightful***
	anapest	- - /	***intertwine***
	amphimacer	/ - /	***come along***

4 Foot Meters are called ***paeons.*** The **First Paeon** is defined as having the first heavy stress of the four syllable unit on the first syllable:

/ - - - / - - - / - - - etc.

The **Second** as having the first heavy stress on the second syllable:

- / - - - / - - - / - -

The **Third** having the stress on the third syllable:

- - / - - - / - - - / -

And the **Fourth,** the stress on the fourth syllable:

- - - / - - - / - - - /

Paeons are not used by Shakespeare though the following line from one of his songs could be scanned as a **Fourth Paeon**

- - - / - - - /

'Hark, hark, the lark at heav'n's gate sings
(Cymbeline
Act II Scene 3)

(Note: This is the rhythm Beethoven establishes at the opening of his 5th Symphony)

Metrical foot: One unit of one of the patterns of light and heavy stress described above (i.e. one **iamb**, one **amphibrach**, etc.) Shakespeare used **trimeter** and **tetrameter** in his jingles, song lyrics, incantations and epilogues (occasionally). His predominate meter was **pentameter**, the meter of the Elizabethan blank verse line, and the one that gives the language its most natural sound.

Line with 3 metrical feet = **trimeter**

Under the greenwood tree
Who loves to lie with me
And tune his merry note
Unto the sweet bird's throat
(*As You Like It Song*
Act II Scene 5)

Line with 4 metrical feet = **tetrameter**

I will drain him dry as hay
Sleep shall neither night nor day
Hang upon his penthouse lid
He shall live a man forbid. . .

(Macbeth Witch's curse
Act I Scene 3)

Line with 5 metrical feet = **pentameter**

Shall I compare thee to a summer's day
Thou art more lovely and more temperate. . .
(Sonnet #18)

Line with 6 metrical feet = **hexameter**

Common in Greek and Latin literature, not used by Shakespeare as its very strict rhythmic pattern (first five feet **dactyls** or **spondees**, sixth usually **dactylic** but occasionally a **spondee)** make it difficult to use, as English has few s**pondees**. An adaptation of the classical **hexameter** is found in Longfellow's *Evangeline:*

/ - - / - - / - - / - - / - - / /
This is the forest primeval, the murmuring pines and the hemlocks…

If the six feet are **iambics (- /),** the resultant twelve-syllable **hexameter** line is called an alexandrine, the favorite rhythm of the French neo-classic dramatists.

Line with 7 metrical feet = **heptameter**

Common in pre-Shakespearean English drama where it was called 'the fourteener', it easily split into a **tetrameter** plus **trimiter,** a rhythm too jingly in its rigid iambics for serious dramatic expression. Shakespeare used it comically in the Pyramus and Thisbe play in *A Midsummer Night's Dream:*

Bottom:
\- / - / - / - / - / -
But stay, oh spite, but mark, poor knight, what dreadful
/ - /
dole is here
Eyes, can you see? How can it be? Oh dainty duck, oh dear!'
(A Midsummer Night's Dream Act 5)

Onomatopoeia: [Greek, *onomatos*, a name, and *poiein*, to make]

Words where the sound of the word echoes or expresses what the word means. 'Pow', 'crash', 'buzz' are common modern examples. In Shakespeare powerful visual images are created or are reinforced the sound of words which echo the thing to which they are referring:

> *King Henry:*
> *<u>Swilled</u> by the wild and wasteful <u>ocean</u>. . .*
> *(Henry V*
> *Act III Scene 1)*
>
> *Petruchio:*
> *Should be? Should <u>buzz</u>.*
>
> *Katharina:*
> *Well ta'en, and like a <u>buzzard</u>.*
> *(The Taming of the Shrew*
> *Act II Scene 1)*
>
> *Bottom:*
> *The <u>raging rocks</u>*
> *And <u>shivering shocks</u>*
> *Shall <u>break</u> the locks*
> *Of prison-gates;*
> *And Phibbus' car*
> *Shall shine from far*
> *And make and mar*
> *The foolish fates.*
> *(A Midsummer Night's Dream*
> *Act I Scene 2)*

Oxymoron: [Greek, from *oxys*, sharp, and *moros*, dull]

Two words which contradict each other, yet seem to describe a reality:

Romeo:

...O brawling love! O loving hate!
O anything, of nothing first create!
O heavy lightness! Serious vanity!
Misshapen chaos of well-seeming forms!
Feather of lead, bright smoke, cold fire, sick health!
Still-waking sleep, that is not what it is!
(Romeo and Juliet
Act I Scene 1)

Helena:
O devilish-holy fray!
(A Midsummer Night's Dream
Act III Scene 2)

Thersites:
He's grown a very landfish . . .
(Troilus and Cressida
Act III Scene 3)

Paradox: [Greek, from *para*, beyond, and *doxon*, opinion]

A statement seemingly contradictory or unbelievable but that may be true; contrary realities, both of which are true. **Paradox** may exist in language but also in character and situation. Related to **ambiguity**, **irony** and **oxymoron.**

Hamlet:
Ay, truly, for the power of beauty will sooner transform honesty from what it is to a bawd, than the force of honesty can translate beauty into his likeness. This was sometime a paradox, but now the time gives it proof.
(Hamlet
Act III Scene 1)

Macbeth :
I pall in resolution, and begin
To doubt th'equivocation of the fiend
That lies like truth: 'Fear not, till Birnum
wood
Do come to Dunsinane'; and now a wood
Comes toward Dunsinane.
(Macbeth
Act V Scene 4)

Lysander:
Transparent Helena! Nature shows art
That through thy bosom makes me see thy
heart.
(A Midsummer Night's Dream
Act II Scene 2)

Timon:
Thus much of this will make black white, foul
fair,
Wrong right, base noble, old young, coward
valiant. . .
This yellow slave
Will knit and break religions, bless the
accursed,
Make the hoar leprosy adored, place thieves
And give them title, knee, and approbation
With senators on the bench.
(Timon of Athens
Act IV Scene 3)

Parallelism: [Greek, *para*, side by side, and *allelon*, of one another]

Repetitive or matching verbal structures.

Suffolk (aside):
She is beautiful, and therefore to be woo'd;
She is a woman, therefore to be won.
(Henry VI Part 1
Act 5 Scene 3)

York:
Bids't thou me rage? why, now thou hast thy wish:
Wouldst have me weep? why, now thou hast thy will. . .
(Henry VI Part 3
Act 1 Scene 4)

Armado:
Why tough signior? Why tough signior?

Moth:
Why tender juvenal? Why tender juvenal?
(Love's Labour's Lost
Act I Scene 2)

Parenthesis: [Greek, *para,* beside, and *entithenai*, to insert]

Interrupting a sentence with an insertion in order to juxtapose ideas strongly. Sister Miriam Joseph notes that Shakespeare uses **parenthesis** extensively, particularly in his latter plays (SUAL, p57), citing the following examples.

Menenius:
If you'll bestow a small (of what you have little)
Patience awhile . . . .
(Coriolanus
Act I Scene 1)

She notes that the use of parenthesis below heightens the frenzy of Leontes's jealousy:

Leontes:
Ha' you not seen,
Camillo
(But that's past doubt; you have, or your eye-
glass
Is thicker than a cuckold's horn), or heard
(For to a vision so apparent rumour
Cannot be mute) or thought (for cogitation
Resides not in that man that does not think)
My wife is slippery?
(The Winter's Tale
Act I Scene 2)

Miranda:
If by your art – my dearest father—you have
Put the wild waters in this roar—allay them;
The sky, it seems, would pour down stinking
pitch,
But that the sea, mounting to th'welkin's
cheek,
Dashes the fire out. . . .O! I have suffered
With those I saw suffer: A brave vessel,
(Who had no doubt some noble creature in
her!)
Dashed all to pieces: O the cry did knock
Against my very heart . . . .
(The Tempest
Act I Scene 1)

Pedantry: **[Latin, *paedogare,* to educate]**

Showing off one's education or knowledge by the use of high-flown words, or foreign terms.

Shakespeare enjoyed making fun of **pedantry**: Holofernes and Don Armado (*Love's Labour's Lost),* Sir Hugh Evans, (*The Merry Wive of Windsor*), Malvolio (*Twelfth Night*), Polonius and the first Gravedigger (*Hamlet*) all demonstrate **pedantry**.

Holofernes:
The deer was, as you know, in sanguis, blood – ripe as the
pomewater who now hangeth like a jewel
in the eare of caelo, the sky, the welkin, the heaven, it drops on the face of terra, the soil, the land, the earth.
(Love's Labour's Lost
Act IV Scene 2)

Polonius:
Madam, I swear I use no art at all.
That he is mad, 'tis true, 'tis true, 'tis pity
And pity 'tis 'tis true. . .
Mad let us grant him then, and now remains
That we find out the cause of this effect,
Or rather say, the cause of this defect,
For this effect defective comes by cause;
Thus it remains and the remainder thus. . .
(Hamlet
Act II Scene 2)

Armado:
I spoke it, tender juvenal, as a congruent epitheton appertaining to thy young days, which we may nominate tender.
(Love's Labour's Lost
Act I Scene 2)

Personification: **[Latin, *persona*, a person, and *facere,* to make]**

Representing ideas or things in human form or having human characteristics. Shakespeare had an impressive instinct for personifying the elements in the world around him. This is a technique that appears with frequency in his language and heightens greatly its imaginative dimension.

Lieutenant:
The gaudy, blabbing and remorseful day
Is crept into the bosom of the sea;
And now loud-howling wolves arouse the jades
That drag the tragic melancholy night;
Who, with their drowsy, slow and flagging wings,
Clip dead men's graves and from their misty jaws
Breathe foul contagious darkness in the air.
(Henry VI Part 2
Act IV Scene 1)

Gloucester:
Grim-visaged war hath smooth'd his wrinkled front;
And now, instead of mounting barded steeds
To fright the souls of fearful adversaries,
He capers nimbly in a lady's chamber
To the lascivious pleasing of a lute.
(Richard III
Act I Scene 1)

Rumour:
Open your ears; for who of you will stop
The vent of hearing when loud Rumour

speaks?
(Henry IV Part 2
Introduction)

Macbeth:
And all our yesterdays have lighted fools
The way to dusty death.
(Macbeth
Act V Scene 5)

Edgar:
There is a cliff, whose high and bending head
Looks fearfully in the confined deep.
(King Lear
Act IV Scene 1)

Ulysses:
For Time is like a fashionable host
That slightly shakes his parting guest by th'hand
And, with his arms outstretched as he would fly
Grasps in the comer: welcome ever smiles,
And farewell goes out sighing. O, let not virtue seek
Remuneration for the thing it was;
For beauty, wit,
High birth, vigour of bone, desert in service,
Love, friendship, charity, are subject all
To envious and calumniating Time.
(Troilus and Cressida
Act III Scene 3)

Prologue: **[Greek, *pro*, before and *logos*, word]**

A speech directed to the audience at the opening

of a play, used to set up the action to come, to establish mood, to introduce cast of characters, etc. Shakespeare began *Romeo and Juliet, Henry V, Troilus and Cressida, Henry VIII*, and *Pericles* with a speech entitled a **prologue**. He began *The Taming of the Shrew* with a separate scene called the Induction, and opened *Henry IV Part II* with a speech given by the personification of Rumour which acts as a **prologue** but which is called an Induction.Inductions are scenes; **prologue**s are speeches, all of which, in Shakespeare, are written in **verse.**

Chorus:
O for a muse of fire that would ascend
The brightest heaven of invention:
A kingdom for a stage, princes to act,
And monarchs to behold the swelling scene.
Then should the warlike Harry, like himself,
Assume the port of Mars, and at his heels,
Leashed in like hounds, should Famine,
Sword, and Fire
Crouch for employment. But pardon, gentles
all,
The flat, unraised spirits that hath dared
On this unworthy scaffold to bring forth
So great an object. Can this cockpit hold
The vasty fields of France? Or may we cram
Into this wooden O the very casques
That did affright the air at Agincourt?
O, pardon! Since a crooked figure may
Attest in little place a million;
And let us, ciphers to this great accompt,
On your imaginary forces work. . . .
Suppose within the girdle of these walls
Are now confined two mighty monarchies,
Whose high, upreared and abutting fronts

The perilous narrow ocean parts asunder.
Piece out our imperfections with your thoughts:
Into a thousand parts divide one man,
And make imaginary puissance.
Think, when we talk of horses, that you see them
Printing their hoofs i'th' receiving earth:
For 'tis y our thoughts that now must deck our kings,
Carry them here and there: jumping o'er times;
Turning th'accomplishment of many years
Into an hour-glass: for the which supply,
Admit me Chorus to this history;
Who prologue-like your humble patience pray,
Gently to hear, kindly to judge, our play.
(Henry V
Prologue)

Prologue:
Two households, both alike in dignity
In fair Verona where we lay our scene,
From ancient grudge break to new mutiny,
Where civil blood makes civil hands unclean.
From forth the fatal loins of these two foes
A pair of star-crossed lovers take their life
Whose misadventured piteous overthrows
Doth with their death bury their parents' strife.
The fearful passage of their death-marked love,
And the continuance of their parents' rage,
Which, but their children's end, nought could remove,
Is now the two hours' traffic of our stage;

The which if you with patient ears attend,
What here shall miss, our toil shall strive to mend.
(Romeo and Juliet Prologue)

Prose: **[Latin, *prosa* and *oratio,* meaning direct and speech]**

Language not structured into verse form. Shakespeare worked easily between **verse** and **prose**, using the change from one to another to trigger contrast in action, mood or character. A play like *The Merry Wives of Windsor* is thought to have been quickly written because it is primarily in prose. This indicates that Shakespeare might have drafted plays in **prose** first, subsequently versifying them. However, as *The Merry Wives of Windsor* is his only play set in a small town and filled with realistic characters, **prose** may have been his choice for stylistic reasons. The opening scene of *Henry IV Part I* is tightly held in check by its verse structure, whereas the **prose** that starts the next scene immediately suggests the unconstrained life Prince Hal enjoys with Falstaff:

King:
Cousin, on Wednesday next our council we
Will hold at Windsor, so inform the lords:
But come yourself with speed to us again,
For more is to be said and to be done
Than out of anger can be uttered.

Scene 2: London

Falstaff:
Now, Hal, what time of day is it, lad?

Hal:
Thou art so fat-witted with drinking of old sack, and unbuttoning thee after supper, and sleeping upon benches after noon, that thou hast forgotten to demand that truly which thou wouldest truly know. What a devil hast thou to do with the time of the day? Unless hours were cups of sack, and minutes capons, and clocks the tongues of bawds, and dials the signs of leaping-houses, and the blessed sun himself a fair hot wench in flame-colored taffeta, I see no reason why thou shouldst be so superfluous to demand the time of day.
(Henry IV Part I
Act I Scene 2)

Puns: **[Italian, *puntiglio,* fine point, hence a verbal quibble]**

Plays on words having more than one meaning, or words that sound alike.

Her love for whose dear love I rise and fall.
(Sonnet #151)

Warwick:
I'll plant Plantagenet, root him up who dares:
Resolve thee, Richard; claim the English crown.
(Henry VI Part 3
Act 1 Scene 1)

Repartee: **[French, from *repartir*, to return quickly a thrust or a blow]**

Witty word play involving swift comments and quick responses.

Petruchio:
Good morrow, Kate; for that's your name, I hear.

Katharina:
Well have you heard, but something hard of hearing:
They call me Katharina that do talk of me.

Petruchio:
You lie, in faith; for you are call'd plain Kate,
And bonny Kate and sometimes Kate the curst;
But Kate, the prettiest Kate in Christendom
Kate of Kate Hall, my super-dainty Kate,
For dainties are all Kates, and therefore, Kate,
Take this of me, Kate of my consolation;
Hearing thy mildness praised in every town,
Thy virtues spoke of, and thy beauty sounded,
Yet not so deeply as to thee belongs,
Myself am moved to woo thee for my wife.

Katharina:
Moved! in good time: let him that moved you hither
Remove you hence: I knew you at the first
You were a moveable.

Petruchio:
Why, what's a moveable?

Katharina:
A joint-stool.

Petruchio:
Thou hast hit it: come, sit on me.
(The Taming of the Shrew
Act II Scene 1)

Beatrice:
I wonder you will still be talking, Signior Benedick – nobody marks you.

Benedick:
What, my dear lady Disdain! Are you yet living?

Beatrice:
Is it possible Disdain should die, while she hath such meet food to feed it as Signior Benedick? Courtesy itself must convert to disdain, if you come in her presence.

Benedick:
Then is courtesy a turn-coat. But it is certain I am loved of all ladies, only you excepted: and I would I could find it in my heart that I had not a hard heart, for truly I love none.

Beatrice:
A dear happiness to women—they would else have been troubled with a pernicious suitor. I thank God and my cold blood, I am of your humour for that. I had rather hear my dog bark at a crow than a man swear he loves me.

Benedick:
God keep your ladyship still in that mind,

so some gentleman or other shall 'scape a predestinate scratched face.

(Much Ado About Nothing
Act I Scene 1)

Repetition: **[Latin, *repetere*, to seek again, repeat]**

Multiple use of the same words or phrase structures for emphasis.

King Henry:
Woe above woe! grief more than common grief!
O that my death would stay these ruthful deeds!
O pity, pity, gentle heaven, pity!

(Henry VI Part 3
Act II Scene 5)

Bottom [as Pyramus]:
Now die, die, die, die, die.

(A Midsummer Night's Dream
Act V)

Lear:
Never, never, never, never, never.

(King Lear
Act V Scene 4)

Lear:
Then kill, kill, kill, kill, kill.

(King Lear
Act IV Scene 6)

Rhetorical Questions: **[Greek, *rhetorike*, the rhetorical art]**

Interrogative phrases that expect no answer from the listener.

Sir Andrew:
Now, sir, have I met you again? There's for you.
(Twelfth Night
Act IV Scene 1)

Gloucester:
Was ever woman in this humour woo'd?
Was ever woman in this humour won?
I'll have her, but I will not keep her long.
(Richard III
Act 1 Scene 2)

Falstaff:
Dost thou hear? It is my ancient.
(Henry IV Part II
Act 2 Scene 4)

Rhyme: **[Middle-English and Anglo-Saxon, *rime*, a number]**

Identity of sounds most often occurring at the ends of lines of verse; frequently used to indicate the end of a scene in Shakespeare. As a stage director I believe that Shakespeare used these final couplets to effect quick exits: on the first half of the couplet the actors move from center state toward their exit and then leave instantaneously as the second half of the couplet is articulated. It is, in my view, always a directorial mistake to speak the full couplet while far from an exit; it ruins the quick rhythm of Shakespeare's scene structure. The final couplet of scenes should act like a cinematic quick cut, and as one set of actors disappeares quickly, the next come in immediately from another entrance on the last word of the couplet.

Portia:
But come, I'll tell thee all my whole device
When I am in my coach, which stays for us
At the park gate; and therefore make haste
away,
For we must measure twenty miles today.
(Merchant of Venice
Act 3 Scene 4)

Salisbury:
Thy friends are fled to wait upon thy foes,
And crossly to thy good all fortune goes.
(Richard II
Act 2 Scene 3)

Pericles:
Lord Cerimon, we do our longing stay
To hear the rest untold: sir, lead's the way.
(Pericles
Act 5 Scene 3)

Rhyme Royal:

A stanza used in poetry consisting of seven lines of rhymed **iambic pentameter,** the last two a rhymed **couplet**. The usual rhyme scheme is **ababbcc,** and on occasion the seventh line is an Alexandrine (six feet instead of five.) Shakespeare wrote *Venus and Adonis* (his first epic poem) in six-line stanzas, but changed to the Rhyme Royal for his next, *The Rape of Lucrece.* According to William Harmon and C. Hugh Holman in *A Handbook to Literature* (p447), the Rhyme Royal is "the only stanza used by all three poets called the greatest in English -- Chaucer, Shakespeare, and Milton…"

O happiness enjoyed but of a few!
And, if possessed, as soon decayed and done
As is the morning sliver-melting dew
Against the golden splendor of the sun!
An expired date, cancelled ere well begun:
Honor and beauty, in the owner's arms
Are weakly fortressed from a world of harms.

Beauty itself doth of itself persuade
The eyes of me without an orator;
Why needeth then apology be made,
To set for that which is so singular?
Or why is Collatine the publisher
Of that rich jewel he should keep unknown
From thievish ears, because it is his own?
(The Rape of Lucrece Stanzas 4 and 5)

Simile: **[Latin, *similis*, a like thing]**

A comparison where one thing is said to be like another.

Warwick:
<u>Their weapons like to lightning</u> came and went;
<u>Our soldiers, like the night-owl's lazy flight,</u>
Or <u>like an idle thresher with a flail,</u>
Fell gently down, as if they struck their friends.
*(Henry VI Part **3** Act II Scene 1)*

Then <u>my state</u>
<u>Like to the lark</u> at break of day arising
(Sonnet #30)

King Henry:
Thou art like an angel, Kate.
(Henry V
Act 5 Scene 2)

Soliloquy: **[Latin, *solus*, alone, and *loqui*, to speak]**

A speech spoken by a character in a play when he is alone (or thinks he is alone) on stage. Shakespearean **soliloquies** are most often addressed to the audience to intensify focus by involving them in the character's dilemma. See the many famous **soliloquies** in *Hamlet* as examples. Below are others:

Benedick:
This can be no trick. The conference was sadly borne. They have the truth of this from Hero. They seem to pity the lady. It seems her affections have their full bent. Love me! why, it must be requited. I hear how I am censured – they say I will bear myself proudly, if I perceive the love come from her: they say too that she will rather die than give any sign of affection. I did never think to marry. I must not seem proud. Happy are they that hear their detractions, and can put them to mending. They say the lady is fair---'tis a truth, I can bear them witness: and virtuous – 'tis so, I cannot reprove it: and wise, but for loving me – by my troth, 'tis no addition to her wit, nor no great argument of her folly, for I will be horribly in love with her. I may chance have some odd quirks and remnants of wit broken on me, because I have railed so long against marriage: but doth not the

appetite alter? A man loves the meat in his youth that he cannot endure in his age. Shall quips and sentences and these paper bullets of the brain awe a man from the career of his humour? No---the world must be peopled. When I said I would die a bachelor, I did not think I should live till I were married. Here comes Beatrice. By this day she's a fair lady. I do spy some marks of love in her.

(Much Ado About Nothing
Act II Scene 3)

Jessica:
Farewell, good Lancelot.
Alack, what heinous sin is it in me
To be ashamed to be my father's child!
But though I am a daughter to his blood,
I am not to his manners. O Lorenzo,
If thou keep promise, I shall end this strife,
Become a Christian, and thy loving wife.

(The Merchant of Venice
Act II Scene 4)

Macbeth:
Tomorrow and tomorrow and tomorrow
Creeps in this petty pace from day to day
Till the last syllable of recorded time.
And all our yesterdays have lighted fools
The way to dusty death. Out, out, brief candle.
Life's but a walking shadow, a poor player
Who struts and frets his hour upon the stage
And then is heard no more. It is a tale
Told by an idiot, full of sound and fury
Signifying nothing.

(Macbeth
Act V Scene 5)

Sonnet: **[Italian, *sonnetto*, from *sonus*, a sound]**

A brief and concentrated lyric poem, in its purest form consisting of fourteen lines of iambic pentameter most often following a formalized rhyme scheme.

Petrarchan rhyme scheme: abba abba cdcd ee
or cdecdc

Spencerian rhyme scheme: abab bcbc cdcd ee

Shakespearean rhyme scheme: abab cdcd efef gg

When in disgrace with fortune and men's eyes
I all alone beweep my outcast state,
And trouble deaf heaven with my bootless cries,
And look upon myself, and curse my fate,
Wishing me like to one more rich in hope,
Featur'd like him, like him with friends possess'd,
Desiring this man's art, and that man's scope,
With what I most enjoy contented least;
Yet in these thoughts my self almost despising,
Haply I think on thee,-- and then my state,
Like to the lark at break of day arising
From sullen earth, sings hymns at heaven's gate;
For thy sweet love remember'd such wealth brings
That then I scorn to change my state with kings.

(Sonnet #29)

Sonnet structures:

Quatrain: **[French, from *quatre,* four]**

The basic unit of the sonnet is comprised of four lines of iambic pentameter, always rhymed in Shakespeare. Shakespearean **sonnet**s are most often composed of three **quatrain**s plus a rhymed **couplet**.

When to the sessions of sweet, silent thought
I summon up remembrance of things past
I sigh the lack of many a thing I sought
And with old woes new wail my dear time's waste.
(Opening quatrain Sonnet #30)

Shall I compare thee to a summer's day?
Thou art more lovely and more temperate.
Rough winds do shake the darling buds of May
And summer's lease hath all too short a date.
(Opening quatrain Sonnet #18)

Octave: **[Latin, *octavus*, eighth, *octo*, eight]**

The first eight lines or two quatrains of a **sonnet,** especially one written in the Italian style where the structure involves two **quatrains** (the **octave**) introducing and developing an idea followed by a **quatrain** and a **couplet** (the **sestet)** which turns and then gives the sonnet its finish and meaning.

Octave: two quatrains
When in disgrace with fortune and men's eyes

I all alone beweep my outcast state
And trouble deaf heaven with my bootless cries
And look upon myself and curse my fate

Wishing me like to one more rich in hope
Featured like him, like him with friends possessed
Desiring this man's art and that man's scope
With what I most enjoy contented least...'

Yet ----- (Sign of the **Volta** – change is coming)

*(Sonnet #29 – **octave**, or first eight lines)*

Sestet: **[Italian, *sesto*, sixth]**

The final six lines of a sonnet comprising the last quatrain plus the final couplet.

Sestet: final quatrain and couplet
Yet in these thoughts, myself almost despising
Haply I think on thee, and then my state
Like to the lark at break of day arising
From sullen earth sings hymns at heaven's gate.

For thy sweet love remembered such wealth brings
That then I scorn to change my state with kings.

*(Sonnet #29 – **sestet**, or last six lines)*

Couplet: **[French, *couple*, a couple]**

The final two lines, rhyming with each other

Couplet
But if the while I think on thee (dear friend)
All losses are restored and sorrows end.
(Sonnet #30,
Couplet)

Volta: **[Italian, *volta*, a turning]**

The moment when a sonnet turns, either between the **octave** and the **sestet** in Italian structure, or between the three **quatrain**s and the **couplet** in most Shakespearean structures. In *Sonnet 29*, above, the **volta** is marked by the words: *Yet in these thoughts...,* establishing an Italianate **octave/ sestet** structure.

In *Sonnet 30*, on the same theme, the **volta** comes at the end of the twelfth line, the change of idea not happening until the **couplet,** giving the sonnet a three **quatrain/couplet** Shakespearean form:

First quatrain: statement of idea:
When to the sessions of sweet, silent thought
I summon up remembrance of things past
I sigh the lack of many a thing I sought
And with old woes new wail my dear time's waste.

Second quatrain: development of idea:
Then can I drown an eye unused to flow
For precious friends hid in death's dateless night

And weep afresh some long-since cancelled woe
And moan the expense of many a vanished sight.

Third quatrain: further development
Then can I grieve at grievances forgone
And heavily from woe to woe tell o'er
The sad account of fore-bemoaned moan
Which I new pay as if not paid before.

Volta** indicated by the word **But

Couplet: finish and meaning
But if the while I think on thee, dear friend,
All losses are restored and sorrows end.

Some of Shakespeare's most original uses of the sonnet were to include **sonnets** in his plays: *Love's Labors Lost Act IV Scene 3* when each of the four young men have attempted to write poems to their loves, and the sonnets of the king and of Longaville are recited; and in *Romeo and Juliet,* where the **prologue** is a **sonnet**, and, in an even more inspired use, the meeting of Romeo and Juliet is structured as a sonnet:

Romeo: ***first quatrain***
If I profane with my unworthiest hand
This holy shrine, the gentle sin is this:
My lips, two blushing pilgrims, ready stand
To smooth that rough touch with a tender kiss.

Juliet: ***second quatrain***
Good pilgrim you do wrong your hand too much,
Which mannerly devotion shows in this:

For saints have hands that pilgrims' hands do touch,
And palm to palm is holy palmers' kiss.

Romeo: ***third quatrain***
Have not saints lips, and holy palmers too?
Juliet:
Ay, pilgrim, lips that t hey must use in prayer.
Romeo:
Oh then, dear saint, do what hands do,
They pray, grant thou, lest faith turn to despair.

Juliet: ***first line of couplet***
Saints do not move, though grant for prayers' sake.
Romeo: ***second line of couplet***
Then move not, while my prayer's effect I take.

The appearance of **sonnets** in the plays dated between 1592-1595 are cited as evidence when scholars attempt to date the composition of Shakespeare's **Sonnets**.

Stanza: **[Italian, *stanza,* stopping place, from low Latin, room]**

A regular organization of lines, usually rhymed, that repeats frequently.

When that I was and a little tiny boy
With hey, ho, the wind and the rain:
A foolish thing was but a toy
For the rain it raineth every day.

But when I came to man's estate,

With hey, ho, the wind and the rain:
'Gainst knaves and fools men shut their gate
For the rain it raineth every day.

But when I came at last to wive
With hey, ho, the wind and the rain:
By swaggering I could never thrive,
For the rain it raineth every day.

But when I came unto my beds,
With hey, ho, the wind and the rain:
With toss-pots still had drunken heads,
For the rain it raineth every day.

A great while ago the world begun,
With hey, ho, the wind and the rain:
But that's all one, our play is done,
And we'll strive to please you every day.
(Twelfth Night
Act V Scene 1)

Stress: **[Latin, *strictus*, strict]**

Alternation of heavy and light emphasis in syllables or words in phrases. (See **Meter**). The syllables with heavy emphasis (**stress**) are underlined below.

Antonio:
In <u>sooth</u> I <u>know</u> not <u>why</u> I <u>am</u> so <u>sad</u>.
(Merchant of Venice
Act 1 Scene 1)

Claudio:
<u>Ay</u>, but to <u>die,</u> and <u>go</u> we <u>know</u> not <u>where</u>. . .
(Measure for Measure
Act III Scene 1)

Demetrius:
If she cannot entreat, I can compel.
(A Midsummer Night's Dream
Act III Scene 2)

Synonym: **[Greek, *synonymon*, of like meaning]**

Words that mean the same thing. An aspect of Shakespeare's early schooling involved making lists of Latin synonyms. In *Will in the World* (p24) Stephen Greenblatt refers to Erasmas's book called *On Copiousness* where as an exercise in finding synonyms he lists 150 different ways of saying 'Thank you for your letter.'

Love is perjured, murd'rous, bloody, full of
blame
Savage, extreme, rude, cruel, not to trust.
(Sonnet # 129)

Grumio:
He bid me knock him and rap him soundly,
sir. . .

Petruchio:
A senseless villain! Good Hortensio,
I bade the rascal knock upon your gate,
And could not get him for my heart to do it.

Grumio:
Knock at the gate! O heavens! Spake you not these words plain, 'Sirrah, knock me here: rap me here: knock me well, and knock me soundly'? And come you now with 'knocking at the gate'?
(The Taming of the Shrew

Act I Scene 2)

Therefore, you clown, abandon (which is in the vulgar 'leave') the society (which in the boorish is 'company') of this female (which in the common is 'woman): which altogether is, 'abandon the society of this female,; or, clown, thou perishest; or, to thy better understanding, diest? Or, to wit, I kill thee. make thee away, translate thy live into death, thy liberty into bondage: I will deal in poison with thee, or in bastinado, or in steel; I will bandy with thee in faction; I will o'er-run thee with policy; I will kill thee a hundred and fifty ways –therefore tremble and depart.
(As You Like It
Act V Scene 1)

Verse: **[Latin, *versus*, a turning, a line or row; turning to begin a new line]**

Metered and often rhymed organization of language. Shakespeare's plays are all a varying mixture of **verse** and **prose**.

Prospero:
Our revels now are ended. . . These our actors
As I foretold you, were all spirits, and
Are melted into air, into thin air,
And, like the baseless fabric of this visio
The cloud-capped towers, the gorgeous palaces,
The solemn temples, the great globe itself,
Yea, all which it inherit, shall dissolve,
And, like this insubstantial pageant faded,
Leave not a rack behind: we are such stuff
As dreams are mad on; and our little life
Is rounded with a sleep.

(The Tempest
Act IV Scene 1)

Now I but chide: but I should use thee worse,
For thou, I fear, hast given me cause to curse. . .
If thou hast slain Lysander in his sleep,
Being o'er shoes in blood, plunge in the deep,
kill me too.
The sun was not so true unto the day
As he to me. Would he have stolen away
From sleeping Hermia? I'll believe as soon
This whole earth may be bored, and that the
moon
May through the centre creep, and so
displease
Her brother's noontide with th'Antipodes.
It cannot be but thou hast murd'red him –
So should a murderer look, so dead, so grim.
(A Midsummer Night's Dream
Act III Scene 2)

Sometimes **verse** is used as a synonym for **stanza**.

Part 2:
Less Familiar Rhetorical Terms

A number of the terms listed below appear in George Puttenham's *Arte of English Poesie*, 1589. By giving the Greek or Latinate terms English equivalents, it would seem Puttenham was trying to make the classical figures of speech easier for the English speaking student to understand and remember. Shakespeare had probably left school by 1580 so he would only have become acquainted with these English terms as an adult, but the names are so charming that when they exist for the terms below I've included them, listed as **'Puttenham's term'** in bold face, keeping his idiosyncratic spelling and capitalizations.

Accismus: **[a KIS mus; Greek, *akkismos*, coyness]**

A false refusal that is hypocritical or insincere.

In *Richard III* (an early play) Shakespeare shows Richard orchestrating a scene to show himself rejecting the offer of the crown in order to demonstrate (false) humility. Thus he hopes to win over a hostile populace.

Buckingham:
Then, good my lord, take to your royal self
This proffered benefit of dignity;
If not to bless us and the land withal,
Yet to draw forth your noble ancestry
From the corruption of abusing times
Unto a lineal true-derived course.

Mayor:

Do, good my lord, your citizens entreat you.

Buckingham:
Refuse not, mighty lord, this proffered love.

Catesby:
O, make them joyful, grant their lawful suit!

Gloucester:
Alas, why would you heap this care on me?
<u>I am unfit for state and majesty</u>:
I do beseech you, take it not amiss;
<u>I cannot nor I will not yield to you.</u>
(Richard III
Act III Scene 7)

Of course, immediately Richard does "yield".

In *Julius Caesar*, we hear about Caesar's **accismus** from the report of Casca.

Casca:
I saw Mark Antony offer him a crown, yet 'twas not a crown neither, 'twas one of these coronets: and, as I told you, he put it by once: but for all that, to my thinking, he would fain have had it. Then he offered it to him again; then he put it by again: but to my thinking, he was very loath to lay his fingers off it. And then he offered it the third time; he put it the third time by: and still as he refused it, the rabblement hooted and clapped their chopped hands and threw up their sweaty night-caps and uttered such a deal of stinking breath because Caesar refused the crown, that it had almost choked Caesar for he swooned and fell down at it: and for mine

> *own part, I durst not laugh, for fear of*
> *opening my lips and receiving the bad air.*
> *(Julius Caesar*
> *Act I Scene 2)*

Shakespeare enjoyed variations on traditional figures. In *Richard II* the **accismus** is within Richard himself. He claims to want to give Bolingbroke the crown but in reality is loathe to give it up. He rejects giving rather than rejects taking.

> *Richard:*
> *Give me the crown . . . .Here, <u>cousin, seize the crown</u>:*
> *Here, cousin,*
> *On this side my hand, and on that side, thine. .*
> *Now is this golden crown like a deep well*
> *That owes two buckets, filling one another,*
> *The emptier ever dancing in the air,*
> *The other down, unseen, and full of water:*
> *That bucket down, and full of tears, am I,*
> *Drinking my griefs, whilst you mount up on high.*
>
> *Bolingbroke:*
> *I thought you had been willing to resign.*
>
> *Richard:*
> *My crown I am, but still my griefs are mine:*
> *You may my glories and my state depose,*
> *But not my griefs, still am I king of those.*
>
> *Bolingbroke:*
> *Part of your cares you give me with your crown.*

Richard:
Your cares set up do not pluck my cares down. . . .

Bolingbroke:
Are you contented to resign the crown?

Richard:
Ay, no; no, ay; for I must nothing be. . .
(Richard II
Act 4 Scene 1)

For an analysis on the subtle word-play on 'ay' and 'I', see **Antanaclasis** below.

Acyron: **[a KAI ron; Greek, *akyrologia*; *a*, priv. and *kyros*, authority]**

A kind of **catacresis**, or misuse of words, where the word used means the opposite of the word intended. One of the vices of language Shakespeare was taught not to use in school, but of which he made great use in creating many of his comedic characters.

Lancelot:
My young master doth expect your reproach. [for approach]
(The Merchant of Venice
Act II Scene 5)

Slender:
I will marry her, sir, at your request; but if there be no great love in the beginning, yet heaven may decrease [for increase] *it upon better acquaintance, . . . if you say, 'Marry her,' I will marry her. That I am freely*

dissolved, and dissolutely. [for resolved and resolutely]

(The Merry Wives of Windsor Act I Scene 1)

In the above example, the first instance is clearly an **acyron,** the subsequent ones examples of **catachresis,** 'dissolved' and 'dissolutely' being misused, but not exactly the opposite of 'resolved' and 'resolutely'. Dogberry is the character with whom Shakespeare uses **acyron** most exuberantly:

Dogberry:
First, who think you the most desartless [for deserving] man to be constable?
(Much Ado About Nothing Act III Scene 3)

You are thought here to be the most senseless and fit men for the constable of the watch.
(Act II Scene 2)

O villarn! thou wilt be condemn'd into everlasting redemption for this!
(Act IV Scene 2)

Allegoria: **[a le GOR ia; Greek, *allegoria*, from *allos*, other and *agoreuein*, to speak in public]**

(Puttenham's term: 'the False Semblant')

A long and perpetual metaphor; also the extension of a **metaphor** to entire long speeches. Three of the four **allegories** below compare the world to a garden, one of Shakespeare's favorite analogies.

Iago:
<u>Our bodies are our gardens</u>, to the which our wills are gardeners; so that if we will plant nettles or sow lettuce, set hyssop and weed up thyme, supply it with one gender of herbs or distract it with many – either to have it sterile with idleness or manured with industry -- why, the power and corrigible authority of this lies in our wills.

(Othello
Act I Scene 3)

Gardner:
Go, bind thou up yon dangling apricocks,
Which <u>like unruly children</u> make their sire
Stoop with oppression of their prodigal
weight,
Give supportance to the bending twigs.
<u>Go thou, and like an executioner</u>
<u>Cut off the heads of too fast growing sprays,</u>
<u>That look to lofty in our commonwealth</u> –
All must be even in our government, , , ,
You thus employed, I will go root away
The noisome weeds which without profit suck
The soil's fertility from wholesome flowers.

Man:
Why should we, in the compass of a pale,
Keep law and form and due proportion,
Showing as in a model our firm estate,
When <u>our sea-walled garden, the whole land,</u>
<u>Is full of weeds, her fairest flowers choked up,</u>
<u>Her fruit-trees all unpruned, her hedges</u>
<u>ruined,</u>
<u>Her knots disordered, and her wholesome</u>
<u>herbs</u>
<u>Swarming with caterpillars</u>?

Gardner:

Hold thy peace—
He that hath suffered this disordered spring
Hath now himself met with the fall of leaf:
The weeds which his broad-spreading leaves did shelter,
That seemed in eating him to hold him up,
Are plucked up root and all by Bolingbroke—
I mean the Earl of Wiltshire, Bushy, Green.

Man:
What, are they dead?

Gardner:

They are, and Bolingbroke
Hath seized the wasteful king. O! what pity is it
That he had not so trimmed and dressed his land,
As we this garden! We at this time of year
Do wound the bark, the skin of our fruit-trees,
Lest being over-proud in sap and blood
With too much riches it confound itself.
Had he done so to great and growing men,
They might have lived to bear, and he to taste,
Their fruits of duty: superfluous branches
We lop away, that bearing boughs may live:
Had he done so, himself had borne the crown,
Which waste of idle hours hath quite thrown down.

(Richard II
Act III Scene 4)

Richard:
I have been studying how I may compare
This prison where I live unto the world:

And for because the world is populous,
And here is not a creature but myself,
I cannot do it; yet I'll hammer it out.
My brain I'll prove the female to my soul,
My soul the father, and these two beget
A generation of still-breeding thoughts:
And these thoughts people this little world,
In humours like the people of this world:
For no thought is contented: the better sort,
As thoughts of things divine, are intermixed
With scruples, and do set the word itself
Against the word,
As thus: 'Come, little ones', and then again,
'It is as hard to come, as for a camel
To thread the postern of a small needle's eye'. .
Thoughts tending to ambition, they do plot
Unlikely wonders: how these vain weak nails
May tear a passage through the flinty ribs
Of this hard world, my ragged prison walls,
And for they cannot, die in their own pride.
(Richard II
Act V Scene 5)

Burgundy:
Great kings of France and England . . . .
let it not disgrace me
If I demand before this royal view
What rub, or what impediment there is,
Why that the naked, poor, and mangled
Peace,
Dear nurse of arts, plenties, and joyful births,
Should not in this best garden of the world,
Our fertile France, put up her lovely visage?
Alas she hath from France too long been
chased,
And all her husbandry doth lie on heaps,
Corrupting in its own fertility.

Her vine, the merry cheerer of the heart,
Unpruned, dies; her hedges, even-pleached,
Like prisoners wildly over-grown with hair,
Put forth disordered twigs: her fallow leas
The darnel, hemlock, and rank fumitory
Doth root upon; while that the coulter rusts,
That should deracinate such savagery:
The even mead, that erst brought sweetly forth
The freckled cowslip, burnet, and green clover,
Wanting the scythe, all uncorrected, rank,
Conceives by idleness, and nothing teems
But hateful docks, rough thistles, kecksies, burs
Losing both beauty and utility;
And as our vineyards, fallows, meads, and hedges
Defective in their natures, grow to wildness,
Even so our houses, and ourselves, and children,
Have lost or do not learn, for want of time,
The sciences that should become our country;
But grow like savages, as soldiers will,
That nothing do but meditate on blood,
To swearing, and stern looks, diffused attire,
And everything that seems unnatural.
Which to reduce into our former favour,
You are assembled: and my speech entreats,
That I may know the let, why gentle Peace
Should not expel these inconveniences,
And bless us with her former qualities.
(Henry V
Act V Scene 2)

From this constant and repetitious use of gardens and flowers in his allegories one concludes that Shakespeare himself knew and loved flowers and gardens. We can be grateful that though his great house New Place was destroyed the lovely garden there remains.

Amphibologia: [am fi bo LO gia; Greek, *amphibolos*, doubtful, and *logia*, from *legein*, to speak]

(Puttenham's term: 'the Ambiguous' or 'the Sense Incertaine')

A type of **ambiguity** or **irony** found when statements are made capable of two different meanings. Sister Miriam Joseph identifies this as "an ambiguity of grammatical structure, often occasioned by a mispunctuation," (*SUAL* p66), while Puttenham says it exists "when we speake or write doubtfully and that the sense may be taken in two ways."

Cassio:
Dost thou hear, my honest friend?

Clown:
No, I hear not your honest friend. I hear you.
(Othello
Act III Scene 1)

Peter Quince:
If we offend, it is with our good will.
That you should think, we come not to offend,
But with good will. To show our simple skill,
That is the true beginning of our end.
Consider then, we come but in despite.
We do not come as minding to content you
Our true intent is. All for your delight,
We are not here. That you should here repent you,

The actors are at hand: and by their show,
You shall know all, that you are need to know.
(A Midsummer Night's Dream
Act V Scene 1)

Anacoenosis: [a na koe NO sis; Greek, *anakoinosis,* to make common]

A rhetorical figure where a speaker asks for an opinion about the point of a debate by appealing to his hearers, or to someone absent, or to the audience. **Anacoenosis** is a kind of **apostrophe**.

Macbeth:
Who can impress the forest, bid the tree
Unfix his earth-bound rout? Sweet bodements! Good.
Rebellious dead, rise never, till the wood
Of Birnam rise, and our high-placed Macbeth
Shall live the lease of nature, pay his breath
To time and mortal custom. Yet my heart
Throbs to know one thing; tell me, if your art
Can tell so much: shall Banquo's issue ever
Reign in this kingdom?
(Macbeth
Act IV Scene 1)

Mark Antony:
If you have tears, prepare to shed them now.
You all do know this mantle: I remember
The first time ever Caesar put it on;
'Twas on a summer's evening, in his tent,
That day he overcame the Nervii:
Look, in this place ran Cassius' dagger through:

See what a rent the envious Casca made:
Through this the well-beloved Brutus
stabbed;
And as he plucked his cursed steel away,
Mark how the blood of Caesar followed it,
As rushing out of doors, to be resolved
If Brutus so unkindly knocked, or no:
For Brutus, as you know, was Caesar's
angel:
Judge, O you gods, how dearly Caesar
loved him!
This was the most unkindest cut of all;
For when the noble Caesar saw him stab,
Ingratitude, more strong than traitor's
arms,
Quite vanquished him: then burst his mighty
heart;
And, in his mantle muffling up his face,
Even at the base of Pompey's statua
(Which all the while ran blood), great
Caesar fell.
O, what a fall was there, my countrymen!
Then I and you and all of us fell down,
Whilst bloody Treason flourished over us.
O, now you weep, and I perceive you feel
The dint of pity: these are gracious drops.
Kind souls, what weep you when you but
behold
Our Caesar's vesture wounded? Look you
here,
Here is himself, marred, as you see, with
traitors.

(Julius Caesar
Act III Scene 2)

Williams:
Under what captain serve you?

Henry (disguised)
Under Sir Thomas Erpingham.

Williams:
A good old commander, and a most kind gentleman: <u>I pray you</u>, <u>what thinks he of our estate</u>?

Henry:
Even as men wracked upon a sand, that look to be washed off the next tide.

Williams:
He hath not told his thought to the king?

Henry:
No: nor it is not meet he should: for, though I speak it to you, I think the king is but a man, as I am: the violet smells to him as it doth to me; the element shows to him as it doth to me; all his senses have but human conditions. . . .

(Henry V
Act IV Scene 1)

Hermione:
Now, <u>my liege,</u>
<u>Tell me</u> what blessings I have here alive
That I should fear to die.
(The Winter's Tale
Act III Scene 2)

Anacoluthon: [an a ko LU thon; Greek, *anakolouthus,* wanting sequence, not following]

A device in which there is a change from one

grammatical structure to another within the same sentence. Allied to **aposiopesis**, a sudden breaking off in mid-sentence.

In the introduction to Charles Isaac Elton's *William Shakespeare His Family and Friends* we read on page 5: "he [Shakespeare] was capable of chuckling with delight over an exact reproduction of a Thucydidean 'anacoluthon.'"

This lack of grammatical sequence is used repeatedly as Benedick, in the following speech, tries to deal with the news that Beatrice loves him.

> *Benedick:*
> *This can be no trick. The conference was sadly borne. They have the truth of this from Hero. They seem to pity the lady. it seems her affections have their full bent. Love me! why, it must be requited. I hear how I am censured—they say I will bear myself proudly, if I perceive the love come from her. . . . They say the lady is fair--- 'tis a truth, I can bear them witness: and virtuous— 'tis so, I cannot reprove it: and wise, but for loving me –by my troth, it is no addition to her wit, nor no great argument of her folly, for I will be horribly in love with her. I may chance have some odd quirks and remnants of wit broken on me because I have railed so long against marriage: but doth not the appetite alter? A man loves the meat in his youth that he cnnot endure in his age. Shall quips and sentences and these paper bullets of the brain awe a man from the career of his humour? No— the world must be peopled.*
>
> *(Much Ado About Nothing Act II Scene 3)*

Though she could not have named it or defined it, the Nurse uses **anacoluthon** (as well as **polysyndeton**) to tease Juliet by delaying news of Romeo.

> *Nurse:*
> *Your love says, like an honest gentleman, and a courteous and a kind, and a handsome, and, I warrant, a virtuous -- Where is your mother?*
> *(Romeo and Juliet*
> *Act II Scene 5)*

And the use of **anacoluthon** movingly demonstrates Ophelia's madness:

> *Ophelia:*
> *They bore him barefaced on the bier,*
> *Hey non nonny, nonny, hey nonny.*
> *And in his grave rained many a tear* –
> *Fare you well, my dove!*
>
> *Laertes:*
> *Hadst thou thy wits, and didst persuade*
> *revenge,*
> *It could not move thus.*
>
> *Ophelia:*
> *You must sing, 'Adown adown,' any you call him adown-a. O, how the wheel becomes it! It is the false steward that stole his master's daughter.*
>
> *Laertes:*
> *This nothing's more than matter.*

Ophelia: [to Laertes]
There's rosemary, that's for remembrance—pray you, love, remember--- And there's pansies, that's for thoughts. . .[to the King] There's fennel for you, and columbines. [to the Queen] There's rue for you , and here's some for me, we may call it herb of grace 'o Sundays—O you must wear your rue with a difference. There's a daisy. I would give you some violets, but they withered all, when my father died—they say he made a good end—[sings] For bonny sweet Robin is all my joy—

Imogen:
O for a horse with wings! Hear'st thou, Pisanio?
He is at Milford Haven. Read, and tell me
How far 'tis thither. If one of mean affairs
May plod it in a week, why may not I
Glide thither in a day? Then true Pisanio,
Who long'st like me to see thy lord, who long'st—
O let me bate—but not like me—yet long'st,
But in fainter kind—O, not like me,
For mine's beyond beyond; say, and speak thick—
Love's counselor should fill the bores of hearing
To the smothering of sense—how far it is
To this same blessed Milford.
(Cymbeline
Act III Scene 2)

Anacrusis: [an a KRU sis; Greek, *anakrousis*, to strike back, *ana*, up, back, and *krouein*, to strike]

An unaccented syllable at the beginning of the line before the regular rhythm of the line is established an upward or back beat. Wright says (*SMA*, p170) ". . . trisyllabic openings in Shakespeare are meant to show a hurried pronunciation of several syllables, even to the point of slurring. Most often the first two syllables lead up to a very important third one:

Or we'll burst them open, if that you come not quickly.
(Henry IV Part I
Act I Scene 3)

And so riveted with faith unto your flesh
(Merchant of Venice
Act V Scene 1)

Let's be sacrificers, but not butchers, Caius.
(Julius Caesar
Act II Scene 1)

Not a word, a word, we stand upon our manners.
(The Winter's Tale
Act IV Scene 4)

Shakespeare uses this form sparingly. When it appears, it evidently signals quick, strong speech, not the lightness or languor typically conveyed by nineteenth-century **anapests**."

Anadiplosis: **[an a di PLO sis; Greek, *anadiploun*, to double; ana, up, again and *diploos,* double]**

(Puttenham's term: 'the Redouble')

Words ending one clause or line used to begin the

one following. Shakespeare uses this figure often; it has the effect of tightening dialogue, quickening pace, and building tension in relationships. In this way **anadiplosis** is akin to **stichomythia.**

Hortensio:
'Tis well; and I have met a gentleman
Hath promised me to help me to another,
A fine musician to instruct our mistress;
So shall I no whit be behind in duty
To fair Bianca, so beloved of me.

Gremio:
Beloved of me; and that my deeds shall prove.
(Taming of the Shrew
Act I Scene 2)

Richard:
I grant thee.

Anne:
Dost grant me, hedgehog?
(Richard III
Act I Scene 2)

Helena:
. . .then be content.
Lysander:
Content with Hermia?
(A Midsummer Night's Dream
Act II Scene 2)

Anaphora: **[a NA fo ra; Greek, *anaphorein*, to carry up or back]**

The same word used to begin successive clauses

or sentences. Contrast with **epistrophe,** where the same word ends a sequence of clauses, and **symploce** which is a combination of the two; **anaphora** is favorite figure of repetition with Shakespeare, and one which has a particularly musical quality.

Warwick:
Between two hawks, which flies the higher pitch;
Between two dogs, which hath the deeper mouth;
Between two blades, which bears the better temper:
Between two horses, which doth bear him best;
Between two girls, which hath the merriest eye;
I have perhaps some shallow spirit of judgment
But in these nice sharp quillets of the law,
Good faith, I am no wiser than a daw.
(Henry VI Part 1
Act II Scene 4)

King Henry:
O God! methinks it were a happy life,
To be no better than a homely swain;
To sit upon a hill, as I do now,
To carve out dials quaintly, point by point,
Thereby to see the minutes how they run,
How many make the hour full complete;
How many hours bring about the day;
How many days will finish up the year;
How many years a mortal man may live.
When this is known, then to divide the times:
So many hours must I tend my flock;

So many hours must I take my rest;
So many hours must I contemplate;
So many hours must I sport myself;
So many days my ewes have been with young;
So many weeks ere the poor fools will ean:
So many years ere I shall shear the fleece:
So minutes, hours, days, months, and years,
Pass'd over to the end they were created,
Would bring white hairs unto a quiet grave
(Henry VI Part 3
Act II Scene 5)

Warwick:
Did I forget that by the house of York
My father came untimely to his death?
Did I let pass the abuse done to my niece?
Did I impale him with the regal crown?
Did I put Henry from his native right?
(Henry VI part 3
Act III Scene 3)

Hermia:
I swear to thee by Cupid's strongest bow,
By his best arrow with the golden head,
By the simplicity of Venus' doves,
By that which knitteth souls and prospers loves. . .
(A Midsummer Night's Dream
Act I Scene 1)

Anastrophe: [a NAS tro fe ; Greek, *anastrophe*, a turning or inversion, from *ana*, back and *strephein*, to turn]

An inversion of the usual order of the parts of a sentence such as 'Back she ran' for 'she ran back.' **Hysteron proteron** (putting the last first) is a kind of **anastrophe** as is **tmisis** (placing words between a compound word).

Ariel:
Jove's lightning, the precursors
O'th' dreadful thunderclaps, more
momentary
And sight-outrunning were not.
(The Tempest
Act I Scene 2)

Prospero:
I'll resolve you--
Which to you shall seem probable--of every
These happen'd accidents.
(The Tempest
Act V Scene 1)

Othello:
Yet I'll not shed her blood,
Nor scar that whiter skin of hers than snow.
(Othello
(Act V Scene 2)

Antanaclasis: [an tan a KLA sis; Greek, *antanaklasis*, a bending back against; anti, against, *anaklan,* to bend back]

(Puttenham's term: 'the Rebound')

Playing with one word written the same but carrying a different sense. The second use of the word 'rebounds' against the first. Sister Miriam Joseph says "**Antanaclasis** depends for its effect on the two or more meanings attached to the same repeated word." (*SUAL* p340) It is therefore the simplest kind of pun. Other punning figures include **asteismus**, a figure shared between two speakers, where one picks up on a word from the first speaker and throws it back with an unexpected meaning and **paronomasia**: words which sound almost alike but carry different meanings.

Isabella:
I am a woeful suitor to your honour,
Please but your honour hear me.
(Measure for Measure
Act II Scene 2)

So thou being rich in will, add to thy will
One will of mine.
(Sonnet #135)

Egeus:
Thou hast by moonlight at her window sung
With faining voice verses of feigning love. . .
(A Midsummer Night's Dream
Act I Scene 1)

Then thou, whose shadow shadows doth make bright,
How would thy shadow's form form happy show
To the clear day with thy much clearer light,
When to unseeing eyes thy shade shines so!
(Sonnet #43)

2 Senator:
If thy revenges hunger for that food
Which nature loathes – take thou the destin'd tenth
And by the hazard of the spotted die
Let die the spotted.
(Timon of Athens

Act V Scene 4)

Mercutio:
Ask for me tomorrow and you will find me a grave man.
(Romeo and Juliet Act III Scene 1)

The example below of **accismus** is also an example, in Richard's answer, of a particularly subtle play on the word 'ay'. Richard immediately as he speaks 'Ay' also hears the word 'I', an **antanaclasis** which takes him to thoughts of his own loss of identity if he gives up the crown.

Bolingbroke:
Are you contented to resign the crown?

Richard:
Ay, no; no, ay; for I must nothing be. . .
(Richard II Act IV Scene 1)

Antanagoge: [an ta a GO ge; Greek, *antanagoge,* a leading or bringing up]

(Puttenham's term: 'the Recompencer')

Balancing a criticism with a compensatory positive. and sometimes the reverse.

Corin:
And how like you this shepherd's life, Master Touchstone?

Touchstone:

Truly, shepherd, in respect of itself, it is a good life; but in respect that it is a shepherd's life, it is naught. In respect that it is solitary, I like it very well; but in respect that it is private, it is a very vile life. Now in respect it is in the fields, it pleaseth me well but in respect it is not in the court, it is tedious. As it is a spare life, look you, it fits my humour well; but as there is no more plenty in it, it goes much against my stomach.

(As You Like It
Act III Scene 2)

Falstaff:
My lord, the man I know. . . But to say I know more harm in him than in myself, were to say more than I know: that he is old, the more the pity, his white hairs do witness it, but that he is, saving your reverence, a whore-master, that I utterly deny: if sack and sugar be a fault, God help the wicked! If to be old and merry be a sin, then many an old host that I know is damned: if to be fat is be to be hated, then Pharaoh's lean kine are to be loved, No, my good lord – banish Peto, banish Bardoplh, banish Poins, but for sweet Jack Falstaff, kind Jack Falstaff, true Jack Falstaff, valiant Jack Falstaff, and therefore more valiant being as he is old Jack Falstaff, banish not him thy Harry's company, banish not him thy Harry's company, banish plump Jack, and banish all the world.

(Henry IV Part I
Act II Scene 4)

Phebe:
'Tis but a peevish boy; yet he talks well.

But what care I for words? Yet words do well
When he that speaks them pleases those that
hear. . . .
But sure he's proud; and yet his pride
becomes him. . .
(As You Like It
Act III Scene 5)

Anthimeria also Enallage [an thi MER i a; Greek, *anti*, against and *meros*, part]

Substituting one part of speech for another: singular for plural, noun for verb, adjective for noun, etc. This figure gives vigor and freshness to the language. Actor awareness and stress on the words substituted will make the usages ring with originality and will allow audiences to appreciate their creativity and expressiveness.

Adjective for noun:

And every fair from fair sometime declines. .
.
(Sonnet # 18)

Noun for verb:

Lear:
. . .the thunder would not peace at my bidding.
(King Lear
Act IV Scene 6)

Lucio:
Lord Angelo dukes it well in his absence.
(Measure for Measure
Act III, Scene 2)

Porter:
I'll <u>devil-porter</u> it no further.
(Macbeth
Act II, Scene 3)

York:
Tut, tut, <u>uncle</u> me no <u>uncle</u> nor <u>but</u> me not
<u>buts</u>
(Richard II
Act II Scene 3)

3 Servant:
<u>Leak'd</u> is our bark,
And we, poor mates, stand on the dying deck
Hearing the surges threat.
(Timon of Athens
Act IV Scene 2)

That use is not forbidden usery
Which <u>happies</u> those that pay the willing loan.
(Sonnet #6)

Nor can I fortune to brief minutes tell,
Pointing to each his thunder, rain, and wind,
Or say with princes if it shall go well
By oft <u>predict</u> that I in heaven find. . .
(Sonnet #14)

Antony:
The hearts
That <u>spanieled</u> me at heels, to whom I gave
Their wishes, do <u>discandy</u>, melt their sweets
On blossoming Caesar –
(Antony and Cleopatra
Act IV Scene 12)

Anthypophora: [an thi PO for a; Greek, *anti*, against and *pherein*, to carry]

(Puttenham's term: 'the Figure of Response')

A rhetorical question, posing a question and answering oneself. Sister Miriam Joseph particularizes the definition further by saying it is a reasoning with ourselves. Most of Shakespeare's soliloquies are filled with **anthypophora**.

2 Commoner:
But indeed sir, we make holiday, to see
Caesar and to rejoice in his triumph.

Marullus:
Wherefore rejoice? What conquest brings he
home?
What tributaries follow him to Rome,
To grace in captive bonds his chariot-wheels?
You blocks, you stones, you worse than
senseless things!
O you hard hearts, you cruel men of Rome,
Knew you not Pompey?
(Julius Caesar
Act I Scene 1)

Mercutio:
Thou? Why thou wilt quarrel with a man that hath a hair more or a hair less in his beard than thou hast. Thou wilt quarrel with a man for cracking nuts, having no other reason but because thou hast hazel eyes. What eye but such and eye would spy our such a quarrel. . . Didst thou not fall out with a tailor for wearing his new doublet before Easter? With another for tying his new shoes with old

riband? And yet thou wilt tutor me from quarrelling?

(Romeo and Juliet
Act III Scene 1)

Gloucester:
Was ever woman in this humour wooed?
Was ever woman in this humour won?
I'll have her, but I will not keep her long.
What! I, that killed her husband and his father,
To take her in her heart's extremest hate,
With curses in her mouth, tears in her eyes,
The bleeding witness of my hatred by;
Having Go, her conscience, and these bars against me
And I no friends to back my suit at all,
But the plain devil and dissembling looks,
And yet to win her! All the world to nothing!
Ha?
Hath she forgot already that brave prince,
Edward, her lord, whom I, some three months since,
Stabbed in my angry mood at Tewkesbury?. .
And will she yet abase her eyes on me,
That cropped the golden prime of this sweet prince,
And made her widow to a woeful bed?
On me, whose all not equals Edward's moiety?
No me, that halts and am misshapen thus?

(Richard III
Act I Scene 2)

Viola:
I left no ring with her. What means this lady?
Fortune forbid my outside have not charmed

<u>her</u>!
She made good view of me, indeed so much
That as methought her eyes had lost her tongue. . .
<u>How will this fadge</u>? <u>My master loves her dearly</u>,
<u>And I (poor monster!) fond as much on him</u>:
And she, mistaken, seems to dote on me:
<u>What will become of this</u>? <u>As I am a man</u>,
<u>My state is desperate for my master's love</u>;
<u>As I am woman</u> – now alas the day! –
<u>What thriftless sighs shall poor Olivia breathe</u>?
<u>O time, thou must untangle this, not I</u>,
It is too hard a knot for me t'untie.
(Twelfth Night Act II Scene 2)

Antimetabole or Chiasmus: [an ti me TA bo le; Greek, *anti*, against, *meta*, beyond and *ballein*, to throw]

(Puttenham's term: 'Countercharge')

Equal structures but with words reversed; the repetition of words in inverted order. **Antimetabole** or **chiasmus** is a kind of **antithesis**, Shakespeare's most important device. If the actor stresses the antithetical word or words in each phrase, the meaning of the line becomes instantly clear.

Oberon:
Some <u>true love turn'd</u> and not <u>a false turn'd true</u>.
(Midsummer Night's Dream Act III Scene 2)

Leontes:
Plainly as heaven sees earth and earth sees heaven.
(The Winter's Tale Act I Scene 2)

Touchstone:
The fool doth think he is wise, but the wise man knows himself to be a fool.
(As You Like It Act V Scene 1)

Benedick:
Till all graces be in one woman, one woman shall not come in my grace.
(Much Ado About Nothing Act II Scene 3)

Viola:
So thou mayst say, the king lies by a beggar, if a beggar dwell near him; or, the church stands by thy tabor, if thy tabor stand by the church.
(Twelfth Night Act III Scene 1)

The expense of spirit in a waste of shame
Is lust in action, and till action, lust
Is perjured, murd'rous, bloody, full of blame....
A bliss in proof, and proved, a very woe
All this the world well knows, yet none knows well
To shun the heaven that leads men to this hell.
(Sonnet #129)

Hermia:
I would my father look'd but with my eyes.

Theseus:
Rather your eyes must with his judgment look.
(A Midsummer Night's Dream
Act I Scene 1)

Coriolanus:
. . .where gentry, title, wisdom
Cannot but conclude but by the yea and no
Of general ignorance – it must omit
Real necessities, and give way the while
To unstable slightness. Purpose so barred, it
follows
Nothing is done to purpose.
(Coriolanus
Act III Scene 1)

Antiphrasis: **[an TIF ra sis; Greek, *antiphrasein*, to express by negation; from *anti*, against. and *phrasein*, to speak]**

(Puttenham's term: 'the Broad flout')

The use of a word or phrase to express the opposite of its apparent meaning; **irony** contained in a single word. In addition to the selections below, see examples in **Irony** listed in **Part I** above.

Antony:
They are all – all -- honorable men.
(Julius Caesar
Act III Scene 2)

Hamlet:
Seems, Madam? Nay, it is: I know not seems.
(Hamlet
Act I Scene 2)

Gloucester:
Simple, plain Clarence! I do love thee so
That I will shortly send thy soul to heaven,
If heaven will take the present at our hands.
(Richard III
Act I Scene 1)

Antisagoge: [an ti sa GO ge; Greek, from *anti,* against and *agein*, to lead – *ago,* I lead]

A figure which unites to an action the promise of a reward, and to its violation, punishment. As this is a key to developing suspense and driving action Shakespeare uses it frequently.

Leontes:
Do't and thou hast the one half of my heart;
Do't not, thou splitt'st thine own.
(The Winter's Tale
Act I Scene 2)

King:
Hamlet comes back, what would you undertake
To show yourself your father's son in deed
More than in words?

Laertes:
To cut his throat I'th' church.

Claudius:
No place indeed should murder sanctuarize,
Revenge should have no bounds: but, good Laertes
Will you do this, keep close within your chamber.

Hamlet returned shall know you are come
home.
We'll put on those shall praise your
excellence,
And set a double varnish on the fame
The Frenchman gave you, bring you in fine
together,
And wager on your heads; he being remiss,
Most generous, and free from all contriving,
Will not peruse the foils, so that with ease,
Or with a little shuffling, you may choose
A sword unbated, and in a pass of practice
Requite him for your father.

Laertes:

I will do't. . . .

King:

<u>If this should fail,</u>
<u>And that our drift look through our bad</u>
<u>performance</u>
<u>'Twere better not assayed.</u> Therefore this
project
Should have a back or second that might
hold,
If this did blast in proof.
(Hamlet
Act IV Scene 7)

Lanham defines **antisagoge** as contrasting evaluations, rewarding the virtuous and punishing the victims, or stating first one side of a proposal than the other. (*HRT* p11)

Caesar:

Cleopatra, know,
We will extenuate rather than enforce:
<u>If you apply yourself to our intents,</u>

Which towards you are most gentle, you shall find
A benefit in this change; but if you seek
To lay on me a cruelty by taking
Antony's course, you shall bereave yourself
Of my good purposes and put your children
To that destruction which I'll guard them from
If thereon you rely.
(Antony and Cleopatra Act V Scene 2)

Sister Miriam Joseph points out the ubiquitous use of **antisagoge** in *Much Ado About Nothing (SUAL* p 161)

Antitheton: **[an TI thi ton; Greek, *anti*, against and *tithenai*, to set]**

(Puttenham's term: 'the Renconter or the Quarreller')

Setting contraries in opposition for heightened contrast. Same as **Antithesis.** See more examples in **Part I** above.

Hamlet:
To be or not to be, that is the question.
Whether 'tis nobler in the mind to suffer
The slings and arrows of outrageous fortune
Or to take arms against a sea of troubles
And by opposing, end them. To die, to sleep .
(Hamlet Act III Scene 1)

Hotspur:
I had rather be a kitten and cry mew

Than one of these same metre ballad-
mongers—
I had rather hear a brazen canstick turned,
Or a dry wheel grate on the axle-tree,
And that would set my teeth nothing on edge,
Nothing so much as mincing poetry –
'Tis like the forced gait of a shuffling nag.
(Henry IV Part I
Act III Scene 1)

Adriana:
I cannot, nor I will not, hold me still.
My tongue, though not my heart, shall have
his will.
(The Comedy of Errors
Act IV Scene 2)

Antonomasia: or **Pariphrasis [an to o MA sia; Greek, *antonomazein*, to call by another name; *anti*, instead of, *onomazein*, to name]**

(Puttenham's term: 'the Surnamer')

Substituting a proper name for an idea it represents, or a patronymic or **epithet** instead of a proper name. Similar to **synecdoche**.

Nestor:
But let the ruffian Boreas [for the north wind]
once enrage
The gentle Thetis [for the sea], *and anon*
behold
The strong-ribbed bark through liquid
mountains cut,
Bounding between the two moist elements
Like Perseus' horse, where's then the saucy
boat,

Whose weak untimbered sides but even now
Corrivaled greatness? Either to harbor fled,
Or made a toast for Neptune [for the sea].
(Troilus and Cressida
Act I Scene 3)

Agamemnon:
Speak, *Prince of Ithaca. . .* [for Ulysses].
(Troilus and Cressida
Act I Scene 3)

Claudius:
And, *England,* [for the King] *if my love thou hold'st at aught --*
As my great power thereof may give thee sense,
Since yet thy cicatrice looks raw and red
After the Danish sword, and thy free awe
Pays homage to us – thou mayst not coldly set
Our sovereign process, which imports at full
By letters congruing to that effect,
The present death of Hamlet. Do it, *England,* [for the King]
For like the hectic in my blood he rages.
(Hamlet
Act IV Scene 3)

Aparithmesis: **[a pa rith ME sis; Greek, to count off, from *apo*, off and *arithmein*, to count]**

See **Enumeratio**

Aphaeresis: **[a FAER e sis; Greek, *apharein*, to take away, from *apo*, away, and *harein*, to take]**

Omitting an initial unstressed syllable: 'neath for beneath; 'mid for amid. The opposite of **elision** (the omission of a final vowel).

Whilst like a willing patient, I will drink
Potions of eisel '<u>gainst</u> my strong infection. . .

(Sonnet 111)

King Henry:
take heed:
For never two such kingdoms did contend
Without much fall of blood, whose guiltless drops
Are every one a woe, a sore complaint
'<u>Gainst</u> him whose wrongs gives edge unto the swords
That makes such waste in brief mortality . . .
(Henry V Act I Scene 1)

Apocope: **[a POK o pe; Greek, *apokopein*, to cut off, *apo*, off and *kopein*, to cut]**

Like **aphaeresis** above and **hypermonosyllable** and **syncope**, below, **apocope** means omitting a sound from a word: 'even' for evening; 'heav'n' for heaven; 'e'en' for even. The capability to include or exclude weak vowel sounds gave Shakespeare and other poets of the time rhythmic flexibility and they used this device freely as needed.

Your love and pity doth th'impression fill,
Which vulgar scandal stamped upon my brow;
For what care I who calls me well or ill,
So you <u>o'er-green</u> my bad, my good allow?
(Sonnet 112)

Helena:
So he dissolved and show'rs of oaths did melt.
(A Midsummer Night's Dream
Act I Scene 2)

Puck:
A lovely boy, stol'n from an Indian king. . .
(A Midsummer Night's Dream
Act II Scene 1)

Hermia:
Being o'er shoes in blood, plunge in the deep
And kill me too.
(A Midsummer Night's Dream
Act III Scene 2)

Aporia: **[a PO ria; Greek, *aporia,* doubt; *apo*, from and *horos*, boundery]**

(Puttenham's term: 'the Doubtfull')

Expressing doubt or deliberation about an issue, often used by Shakespeare to intensify the importance of what is at stake.

King Henry:
My learned lord, we pray you to proceed,
And justly and rightly unfold
Why the law Salic that they have in France
Or should or should not bar us in our claim:
And God forbid, my dear and faithful lord,
That you should fashion, wrest, or bow your
reading,
Or nicely charge your understanding soul
With opening titles miscreate, whose right
Suits not in native colours with the truth:
For God doth know how many now in health

Shall drop their blood in approbation
Of what your reverence shall incite us to.
Therefore take heed how you impawn our person,
How you awake our sleeping sword of war;
We charge you in the name of God, take heed:
For never two such kingdoms did contend
Without much fall of blood, whose guiltless drops
Are every one a woe, a sore complaint
'Gainst him whose wrongs gives edge unto the swords
That makes such waste in brief mortality . . .
May I with right and conscience make this claim?

(Henry V
Act I Scene 2)

Hamlet:

The spirit that I have seen
May be a devil, and the devil hath power
T'assume a pleasing shape, yea, and perhaps
Out of my weakness and my melancholy,
As he is very potent with such spirits,
Abuses me to damn me; I'll have grounds
More relative than this – the play's the thing
Wherein I'll catch the conscience of the king.

(Hamlet
Act II scene 2)

Macbeth:

Prithee, peace:
I dare do all that may become a man;
Who dares do more, is none. . . .
If we should fail?

(Macbeth

Act I Scene 7)

Brutus:
It must be by his death: and, for my part,
I know no personal cause to spurn at him,
But for the general – he would be crowned:
How that might change his nature, there's the question.
It is the bright day that brings forth the adder;
And that craves wary walking. . . Crown him! That!
And then, I grant, we put a sting in him,
That at his will he may do danger with.
(Julius Caesar
Act II Scene 1)

Aposiopesis: [a pa si o PE sis; Greek, *aposiopan,* to be silent; *apo*, from, and *siopan,* to be silent]

(Puttenham's term: 'the Figure of Silence')

The sudden breaking off of a discourse before it is ended; passing over something as if unable or unwilling to tell it. **Puttenham**: **"like the man that serves many masters at once, being of strange Countries or kindreds."**

Aposiopesis frequently if not always results in **anacoluthon** (the abrupt change of grammatical structure within the same sentence)

King Richard:
Some light-foot friend post to the Duke of Norfolk.
Ratcliff, thyself – or Catesby – where is he?
(Richard III
Act. IV Scene 4)

Troilus:
At Priam's royal table do I sit
And when fair Cressid comes into my thoughts
So,traitor! 'When she comes!' – when is she
thence?'
(Troilus and Cressida
Act 1 Scene 1)

Desdemona:
The poor soul sat sighing by a sycamore tree,
Sing all a green willow;
Her hand on her bosom, her head on her
knee,
Sing willow, willow, willow:
The fresh streams ran by her and murmured
her moans;
Sing willow, willow, willow;
Her salt tears fell from her, and softened the
stone –

Lay by these –

Sing willow, willow, willow.
(Othello
Act IV Scene 3)

Portia:
Beshrew your eyes,
They have o'er-looked me and divided me,
One half of me is yours, the other half –
yours—
Mine own I would say: but if mine then yours,
And so all yours.
(Merchant of Venice
Act III Scene 2)

Laurie Maguire, (*WTWTW* p162) analyses Portia's speech as follows: "Note how the intellectual penny drops as she is speaking. We see her change of thought in the structure of her sentence. She starts to say that because she is now 50 percent Bassanio's, she is only 50 percent her own; 'One half of me is yours, the other half mine' is what she intends to say. But she realizes that this is not correct. The repetition of 'yours' clearly comes as a surprise to her, and so she had to provide an explanation: 'One half of me is yours, the other half – yours – Mine own, I would say; but if mine, then yours, and so all yours.'" By these discoveries Shakespeare gives the performer an inhanced ability to stay in the moment – indicated by the use of **aposiopesis.**

Apostrophe: [a POS tro fe; Greek, *apostrephein*, to turn away from; *apo*, from, and *strephein,* to turn]

(Puttenham's term: 'the Turnetale')

A turning away from the subject at hand, as in **aposiopesis** above, but here it is in order to address another entity either present or absent, also defined as a short speech given to absent persons, things or gods. According to **Puttenham**, a sudden turn in a speech then coming back. As this happens when people are caught in particularly dramatic situations, it is a device used often by Shakespeare. For related figures see **Anacoenosis, Aposiopesis,** and **Anacoluthon** above.

Hamlet:

A murderer and a villain,
A slave that is not the twentieth part the tithe

Of your precedent lord, a vice of kings,
A cutpurse of the empire and the rule,
That from a shelf the precious diadem stole
And put it in his pocket –

Queen:
No more.
Hamlet:
A king of shreds and patches ---
(Enter the Ghost in his night-gown)
Save me and hover o'er me with your wings,
You heavenly guards! – what would your gracious figure?

Queen:
Alas, he's mad.
(Hamlet
Act III Scene 4)

Cassius:
Now in the names of all the gods at once,
Upon what meat doth this our Caesar feed
That he hath grown so great? Age, thou are shamed!
Rome, thou hast lost the breed of noble bloods!
(Julius Caesar
Act I Scene 2)

Cleopatra:
O Charmian,
Where think'st thou he is now? Stands he, or sits he?
Or does he walk? Or is he on his horse?
O happy horse, to bear the weight of Antony!
Do bravely, horse!
(Antony and Cleopatra
Act I Scene 5)

Bottom:
But what see I? No Thisby do I see.
<u>O wicked wall</u> through whom I see no bliss
Cursed be thy stones for thus deceiving me.
(A Midsummer Night's Dream
Act 5 Scene 1)

Jaques:
But, for the seventh cause. How did you find the quarrel on the seventh cause?

Touchstone:
Upon a lie seven times removed . . . bear your body more seeming, Audrey. . . as thus, sir: I did dislike the cut of a certain courtier's beard. . .
(As You Like It
Act V Scene 1)

Apothegm: **[AP o them; Greek, apotithenai, to set off, put aside]**

A terse, pointed remark or brief instructive saying; see **Adage** in **Part I.**

Lysander:
<u>The course of true love never did run smooth.</u>
(A Midsummer Night's Dream
Act 1 Scene 1)

Polonius:
<u>Neither a borrower nor a lender be.</u> . . .
<u>This above all, to thine own self be true</u>. . .
(Hamlet
Act I Scene 3)

Caesar:
Cowards die may times before their deaths;
The valiant never taste of death but once.
(Julius Caesar
Act II Scene 2)

Cressida:
Things won are done, joy's soul lies in the
doing. . .
Men prize the thing ungained more than it is. . .
Achievement is command; ungained, beseech.
(Troilus and Cressida
Act I Scene 2)

Asteismus: **[a ste IS mus; Greek, *asteismos*, from *asteios*, of the city, polite; refined witty talk; polite and ingenious mockery]**

(Puttenham's term: 'the Merry Scoffe' or 'the Civil Jest')

The picking up of a word and giving it a different application; often a mocking or facetious answer that plays on a word.

Gloucester:
Ay, good leave have you; for you will have
leave,
Till youth take leave and leave you to the
crutch.
(Henry VI Part 3
Act III Scene 2)

Helena:
For, ere Demetrius look'd on Hermia's eyen,
He hail'd down oaths that he was only mine;
And when this hail some heat from Hermia

felt,
So he dissolv'd and show'rs of oaths did melt.
(A Midsummer Night's Dream
Act I Scene 2)

Bolingbroke:
Convey him to the tower!

Richard II:
Oh good, Convey! Conveyers are you all.
(Richard II
Act IV Scene 1)

2 Senator:
If thy revenges hunger for that food
Which nature loathes – take thou the destin'd
tenth
And by the hazard of the spotted die
Let die the spotted.
(Timon of Athens
Act V Scene 4)

Asyndeton: **[a SYN de ton; Greek, *asyndeton*; *a,* priv. and *syndein,* to bind together] Also called brachylogia**

(Puttenham's term: 'Loose Language' "It is a figure to be used when we will seem to make haste, or to be earnest.")

The omission of an expected conjunction between phrases. B**rachylogia** omits the conjunction between single words. In the following quote the conjunction 'or' is consistently omitted adding urgency to the speech:

Ariel:
All hail, great master! Grave sir, hail! I come

To answer they best pleasure; be't to fly,
To swim, to dive into the fire, to ride
On the curl'd clouds.
(The Tempest
Act I Scene 2)

The example below contains first **asyndeton,** then **brachylogia:**

Ulysses:
But when the planets
In evil mixture to disorder wander,
What plagues, and what portents, what mutiny,
What raging of the sea, shaking of earth,
Commotion in the winds, frights, changes, horrors
Divert and crack, rend and deracinate
The unity and married calm of states. . .
(Troilus and Cressida
Act I Scene 3)

Auxesis: **[aux ES is; Greek, *auxesis*, increase]**

(Puttenham's term: 'the Advancer'; also **incrementum** or **progression)**

Accumulating detail for rhetorical effect, mounting by degrees from less to greater by arranging clauses or words in a sequence of accumulating force. Related to **climax**, below, and sometimes (as in Pethruchio's speech below) to **hyperbole.**

Petruchio:
Think you a little din can daunt mine ears?
Have I not in my time heard lions roar?
Have I not heard the sea puffed up with winds

Rage like an angry boar chafed with sweat?
Have I not heard great ordnance in the field,
And heaven's artillery thunder in the skies?
Have I not in pitched battle heard
Loud 'larums, neighing steeds, and trumpets' clang?
And do you tell me of a woman's tongue,
That gives not half so great a blow to hear,
As will a chestnut in a farmer's fire?
Tush! Tush! Fear boys with bugs.
(Taming of the Shrew Act I Scene 2)

King:
The game's afoot:
Follow your spirit; and upon this charge,
Cry, 'God for Harry, England, and Saint George!'
(Henry V Act III Scene 1)

Gaunt:
This royal throne of kings, this sceptred isle,
This earth of majesty, this seat of Mars,
This other Eden, demi-paradise . . . .
This blessed plot, this earth, this realm, this England . . .
(Richard II Act II Scene 1)

Polonius:
And he, repulsed, a short tale to make,
Fell into a sadness, then into a fast,
Thence to a watch, thence into a weakness,
Thence to a lightness, and, by this declension,
Into the madness wherein now he raves.

(Hamlet
Act II Scene 2)

Barbarismus: [bar bar IS mus; Latin, *barbarus*, Greek, *barbaros*, foreign]

Mispronunciation of English words; foreign speech. Shakespeare makes a point of this in the Welsh accent of Sir Hugh Evans and the French accent of Dr. Caius in *The Merry Wives of Windsor;* in the Irish of MacMorris, the Welsh of Fluellen, the Scots of Jamie, and the French of the Princess and Alice her Lady in Waiting in *Henry V*; the Welsh of Glendower's daughter, Lady Mortimer, who speaks only in Welsh in *Henry IV Part I.*

Fluellen:
It is the greatest admiration in the universal world, when the true and ancient prerogatifes and laws of the wars is not kept: if you would take the pains but to examine the wars of Pompey the Great, you shall find, I warrant you, that there is no tiddle taddle nor pibble pabble in Pompey's camp: I warrant you, you shall find the ceremonies of the wars, and the cares of it,and the forms of it, and the sobriety of it, and the modesty of it, to be otherwise.
(Henry V
Act IV Scene 1)

Caius:
Vat is you sing? I do not like des toys: pray you, go and vetch me in my closet un boitier vert; a box, a green-a box. Do intend wat I speak? A green-a box.
(The Merry Wives of Windsor
Act II Scene 4)

Katharine:
Your majesty shall mock at me, I cannot speak your England. . .
Pardonnyz-moi, I cannot tell vat is 'like me.'. .
(Henry V
Act V Scene 2)

Bomphiologia: [bom fi o LO gi a; Latin bombus, humming noise]

(Puttenham's term: 'Pompous Speech' "Using such bombasted words as seem altogether forced full of winde, being a great deale too high and loftie for the matter.")

A 'vice' of language related to **Cacozelia** below**.** In Shakespeare's hands bombastic speech becomes a rich, imaginative device to establish and heighten comedic characterizations.

Pistol:
'Solus,' egregious dog? O viper vile!
The 'solus' in thy most mervailous face;
The 'solus' in thy teeth, and in thy throat,
And in thy hateful lungs, yea, in thy maw, perdy
And, which is worse, within thy nasty mouth!
I do retort the 'solus' in thy bowels;
For I can take, and pistol's cock is up,
And flashing fire will follow.
(Henry V
Act II Scene 1)

Holofernes:
This is a gift that I have, simple, simple; a foolish extravagant spirit, full of forms,

figures, shapes, objects, ideas, apprehensions, motions, revolutions. These are begot in the ventricle of memory, nourished in the womb of pia mater, and delivered upon the mellowing of occasion. But the gift is good in those in whom it is acute, and I am thankful for it.

(Love's Labour's Lost
Act IV Scene 2)

Viola:
Most excellent accomplished lady, the heavens rain odours on you! . . .
My matter hath no voice, lady, but to your own most pregnant and vouchsafed ear. . .
Cesario is your sevant's name, fair princess.
. *Your servant's servant is your servant madam. . . .I come to whet your gentle thoughts on his behalf.*

(Twelfth Night
Act III Scene 1)

Brachylogia: [bra chi o LO gi a; Greek, brachio, arm, relation to the arm]

(Puttenham's term: 'the Cutted Comma')

"To procede all by single words. In long clauses it is called asyndeton. In both cases we utter in that fashion when either we be in earnest or would seem to make haste."

Note an example of **brachylogia** in the Holofernes speech above. See examples of clauses without conjunctions above under **Asyndeton.**

Paris:
Beguil'd, divorced, wronged, spited, slain!. .

Capulet:
Despis'd, distressed, hated, marty'rd, killed!
(Romeo and Juliet
Act IV Scene 5)

Enobarbus:
Hoo! Hearts, tongues, figures, scribes, bards,
poets, cannot
Think, speak, cast, write, sing, number ---
hoo!—
His love to Antony.
(Antony and Cleopatra
Act III Scene 2)

King Henry:
So minutes, hours, days, months, and years,
Pass'd over to the end they were created,
Would bring white hairs unto a quiet grave.
(Henry VI Part 3
Act II Scene 5)

Egeus:
Thou hast by moonlight at her window sung
With feigning voice verses of feigning love,
And stol'n the impression of her fantasy
With bracelets of thy hair, rings, gauds,
conceits
Knacks, trifles, nosegays, sweetmeats . . .
(A Midsummer Night's Dream
Act I Scene 1)

Cacemphaton: [kak EM fa ton; Greek, *kakemphaton,* ill-sounding, equivocal]

(Puttenham's term: 'the Figure of Foule speeche')

To move to laughter or to make sport with scurrilous speech. For a complete investigation of Shakespeare's use of **cacemphaton** see Eric Partridge's classic book *Shakespeare's Bawdy*.

Hamlet:
Lady, <u>shall I lie in your lap</u>?

Ophelia:
No, my lord.

Hamlet:
I mean with my head upon your lap?

Ophelia:
Ay, my lord.

Hamlet:
Do you think I meant country matters?

Ophelia:
I think nothing, my lord.

Hamlet:
<u>That's a fair thought to lie between maids' legs</u>.

(Hamlet
Act III Scene 2)

Curtis:
Is she so hot a shrew as she's reported?

Grumio:
She was, good Curtis, before this frost: but thou know'st winter tames man, woman and beast; for it hath tamed my old master, and

my new mistress, and myself, fellow Curtis.

Curtis:
Away, you three-inch fool! I am no beast.

Grumio:
Am I but three inches? Why, thy horn is a foot, and so long am I at the least.

(The Taming of the Shrew Act IV Scene 1)

Petruchio:
Come, come, you wasp, i'faith, you are too angry.

Katharina:
If I be waspish, best beware my sting.

Petruchio:
My remedy is, then, to pluck it out.

Katharina:
Ay, if the fool could find it where it lies.

Petruchio:
Who knows not where a wasp doth wear his sting?
In his tail.

Katharina:
In his tongue.

Petruchio:
Whose tongue?

Katharina:
Yours if you talk of tales, and so farewell.

Petruchio:
What, with my tongue in your tail? Nay, come again.
(The Taming of the Shrew Act II Scene 1)

Cacozelia: **[ka ko ZE li a; Greek, *kakozelos*, ill-affected, or badly imitating]**

(Puttenham's term: 'Fonde Affectation')

"When we affect new words and phrases other than the good speakers and writers in any language, or their custome hath allowed."

Reaching too hard to show originality or novelty in speech. This was one of the vices of language, usages to be eschewed. Shakespeare especially enjoyed using this figure to comedic or satiric effect.
Related to **Bomphylogia** above**.**

Osric:
Sir, here is newly come to court Laertes; believe me, an absolute gentleman, full of most excellent differences, of very soft society and great showing. Indeed, to speak feelingly of him, he is the card or calendar of gentry; for you shall find in him the continent of what part a gentlemen would see.

Hamlet:
Sir, his definement suffers no perdition in you; though, I know, to divide him inventorially would dozy th'arithmatic of memory, and yet but yaw neither in respect of his quick sail.

But, in the verity of extolment, I take him to be a soul of great article, and his infusion of such dearth and rareness as, to make true diction of him, his sembable is his mirror . . .
(Hamlet
Act V Scene 2)

Touchstone:
Therefore, you clown, abandon (which is in the vulgar, leave) the society (which in the boorish is, company) of this female (which I the common is, woman); which together is, abandon the society of this female.
(As You Like It
Act V Scene 1)

Mercutio
O, he is the courageous captain of compliments. . . Ah, the immortal passado! The punto reverso!. . .The pox of such antic, lisping fantasticoes – these new tuners of accents!
(Romeo and Juliet
Act II Scene 4)

Armado:
Sir, it is the King's most sweet pleasure and affection to congratulate the Princess at her pavilion in the posteriors of this day, which the rude call the afternoon.

Holofernes:
The posterior of the day, most generous sir, is liable, congruent, and measusrable for the afternoon. The word is well cull'd, chose, sweet, and apt.

(Love's Labour's Lost
Act V Scene 1)

Catachresis: [ka ta KREE sis; Greek, *katachresis,* the misuse of a word; *kata*, against, and *chrestha*, to use]

(Puttenham's term: 'the Figure of Abuse')

The miss-use of words; the classical term for what we now call **malapropism**, after the character Mrs. Malaprop in the 18th century play of Richard Brinsley Sheridan, *The Rivals.*

When the misuse involves using a word contrary to what is meant it is a particular kind of **catachresis** called **acyron**. Dogberry and the Watch in *Much Ado About Nothing* show Shakespeare's delight in developing a character out of the use of this figure.

Dogberry:
This is your charge: <u>you shall comprehend all vagrom men</u>.

<u>Comparisons are odorous</u>.

Only get the learned writer to <u>set down our excommunication</u>, and meet me at the jail.

<u>Dost thou not suspect my place</u>? <u>Dost thou not suspect my years</u>?
(Much Ado About Nothing
Act III Scene 3)

Sir Andrew:
He is the very devil <u>incardinate.</u>

(Twelfth Night
Act V Scene 1)

Chiasmus: **[ki AS mus; Greek, *chiasmos,* placing crosswise; *chiazein* to mark with the letter *chi*]** See **Antimetabole** above.

Chronographia: [kro no GRA fia; Greek, *chronos*, time and *graphein*, to write]

(Puttenham's term: 'the Counterfeit of Time')

Descriptions of the changing of the seasons, the passage of time.

Romeo:
Night's candles are burnt out, and jocund day
Stands tiptoe on the misty Mountain tops.
(Romeo and Juliet
Act III Scene 5)

Hamlet:
The air bites shrewdly, it is very cold.

Horatio:
It is a nipping and an eager air.

Hamlet:
What hour now?

Horatio:
I think it lacks of twelve.

Marcellus:
No, it is struck.
(Hamlet
Act I Scene 4)

That time of year thou mayst in me behold
When yellow leaves, or none, or few do hang
Upon those boughs which shake against the
cold,
Bare ruined choirs, where late the sweet birds
sang.
In me thou seest the twilight of such day,
As after sunset fadeth in the west,
Which by and by black night doth take away,
Death's second self that seals up all in rest.
(Sonnet #73)

Portia:
Peace, ho! The moon sleeps with Endymion
And would not be awaked.
(The Merchant of Venice
Act V Scene 1)

Theseus:
Now, fair Hippolyta, our nuptial hour
Draws on apace: four happy days bring in
Another moon: but O, methinks how slow
This old moon wanes . . . .

Hippolyta:
Four days will quickly steep themselves in
night:
Four nights will quickly dream away the time:
And then the moon, like to a silver bow
New-bent in heaven, shall behold the night
Of our solemnities.
(A Midsummer Night's Dream
Act I Scene 1)

Clymax: **[KLI max; Greek, *klimas*, a ladder, from *klinein*, to slope]**

(Puttenham's term: 'the Marching figure')

According to Sister Miriam Joseph (*SUAL*, p83) **climax** is an extended **anadiplosis**, occurring when the last word of one line becomes the first word of the next through three or more clauses:

Claudius:
And let the kettle to the trumpet speak,
The trumpet to the cannoneer without,
The cannons to the heavens, the heaven to earth.
(Hamlet Act V Scene 2)

For a less restrictive definition of climactic build see **Auxesis** above.

Commoratio: [ko mo RA tio; Latin, abiding, *commomare*, to abide or stay]

(Puttenham's term: 'the Figure of Abode')

Emphasising a strong point by repeating it several times in different words. When the same words are used the figure is called **epimone.** In the example below Desdemona uses **commoratio** while Othello uses **epimone,** creating a frightening insistence, a compulsion foreshadowing his later devastating act.

Desdemona:
Pray you let Cassio be receiv'd again.

Othello:
Fetch me the handkerchief! My mind misgives.

Desdemona:
Come, come!
You'll never meet a more sufficient man.

Othello:
The handkerchief!

Desdemona:
I pray talk me of Cassio.

Othello:
The handkerchief!

Desdemona:
A man that all his time
Hath founded his good fortune on your love,
Shar'd dangers with you –

Othello:
The handkerchief!
(Othello
Act III Scene 4)

Antony:
But here's a parchment with the seal of
Caesar;
I found it in his closet; 'tis his will:
Let but the commons hear this testament—
Which, pardon me, I do not mean to read –
And they would go and kiss dead Caesar's
wounds,
Yea, beg a hair of him for memory,
And, dying mention it within their wills,
Bequeathing it as a rich legacy
Unto their issue.

4 Plebeian:
<u>We'll hear the will</u>: read it, Mark Antony.

All:
<u>The will, the will</u>! We will hear <u>Caesar's will</u>.

Antony:
Have patience, gentle friends, I must not read
it;
It is not meet you know how Caesar loved you
. . .

4 Plebeian:
<u>Read the will</u>; we'll hear it, Antony;
You shall <u>read us the will</u>, <u>Caesar's will</u>.
(Julius Caesar
Act III Scene 2)

Definitio: **[Latin, *definitio,* a boundery, from *definire*, to define]**

Definition attempts to explain the nature of a subject by citing its genus and differences, by telling both what something is and what it is not. For similar constructs see **Diaeresis**, **Eutrepismus, Enumeratio, Merismus**, **Synecdoche**, **Systrophe**, **Synathroesmus (Part II)** and **Synonym (Part I).** Shakespeare refers often to the need to define concepts. Sister Miriam Joseph gives as an example this demand of Armado to his page, Moth:

Armado:
<u>Define, define</u>, well-educated infant.
(Love's Labour's Lost
Act I Scene 2)

Polonius:
to define true madness,
What is't but to be nothing else but mad?
(Hamlet
Act II Scene 2))

Let me not to the marriage of true minds
Admit impediments, love is not love
Which alters when it alteration finds,
Or bends with the remover to remove.
O no, it is an ever-fixed mark
That looks on tempests and is never shaken;
It is the star to every wand'ring bark,
Whose worth's unknown, although his height be taken.
Love's not Time's fool, though rosy lips and cheeks
Within his bending sickle's compass come,
Love alters not with his brief hours and weeks,
But bears it out even to the edge of doom:
(Sonnet #116)

Macbeth:
Out, out, brief candle!
Life's but a walking shadow, a poor player
That struts and frets his hour upon the stage,
And then is heard no more: it is a tale
Told by an idiot, full of sound and fury,
Signifying nothing.
(Macbeth
Act V Scene 5)

Descriptio: [dis KRIP tio; Latin, *describire*, to write down]

To delineate or portray in art. The description of characters according to stereotypical expectations, particularly as concerning national types, i.e. Englishmen described according to how they eat or dress, Dutchmen for drinking, Frenchmen for pride and inconstancy, Spaniards for distain and physical nimbleness, Italians for with and tact, Scotsmen for boldness, etc. (*WS,* Rowse, p78)

King:
. . . our court you know is haunted
With a refined traveler of Spain—
A man in all the world's new fashion planted,
That hath a mint of phrases in his brain:
One who the music of his own vain tongue
Doth ravish like enchanting harmony:
A man of complements, whom right and wrong
Have chose as umpire of their mutiny.
This child of fancy, that Armado hight,
For interim to our studies shall relate
In high-born words the worth of many a knight
From tawny Spain lost in the world's debate.
(Love's Labour's Lost
Act I Scene 1)

Nerissa:
How say you by the <u>French lord,</u> Monsieur Le Bon?

Portia:
God made him, and therefore let him pass for a man – In truth, I know it is a sin to be a mocker, but he! Why, <u>he hath a horse better than the Neapolitan's, a better bad habit of frowning than the Count Palatine</u> – he is <u>every man in no man</u> – <u>if a throstle sing, he falls straight a cap-ring</u>—he will <u>fence with</u>

his own shadow. . . .

Nerissa:
What say you then to Falconbridge, the young baron of England?

Portia:
You know I say nothing to him, for he understands not me, nor I him: he hath neither Latin, French, nor Italian. . . . He is a proper man's picture, but, alas! Who can converse wit h a dumb-show? How oddly he is suited! I think he bought his doublet in Italy, his round hose in France, his bonnet in Germany, and his behaviour every where.

Nerissa:
How like you the young German, the Duke of Saxony's nephew?

Portia:
Very viley in the morning when he is sober and most vilely in the afternoon when he is drunk. . . . Therefore, for fear of the worst, I pray thee set a deep glass of rhenish wine on the contrary casket, for if the devil be within, and that temptation without, I know he will choose it.

(*The Merchant of Venice*
Act 1 Scene 2)

Diacope: **[di A ko pe; Greek, a gash or cleft, from *diakopein*, to cut through]**

Interspersing a word between repeated ones. Another term for **ploce** and **tmesis.** This usage suggests high emotionality as it repeats, then delays, then repeats a crucial word.

Hamlet:
O villain, villain, smiling, damned villain!'
(Hamlet
Act I Scene 5)

Lady Percy:
And him, O wondrous him!
O miracle of men! him did you leave.
(Henry IV Part 2
Act II Scene 3)

Troilus:
O Cressid! O false Cressid! False, false, false.!
(Troilus and Cressida
Act V Scene 2)

Lear:
O let me not be mad, not mad, sweet heaven!
(King Lear
Act I Scene 5)

Diaeresis: **[di AIR e sis; Greek, *diairesis,* from *diairein*, to divide, separate; *dia*, apart and *harein*, to take]**

There are two different definitions for this term: the separation of two consecutive vowels, especially of a diphthong, into two syllables; and the division of a genus into its species – related to **defintion.** The examples below are of the second definition as this is the usage quoted by Sister Miriam Joseph as used by Shakespeare.

Jaques:
I have neither the scholar's melancholy,

which is emulation; nor the musician's, which is fantastical; nor the courtier's, which is proud; nor the soldier's, which is ambitious; nor the lawyer's, which is politic; nor the lady's, which is nice; nor the lover's, which is all these: but it is a melancholy of mine own . . .

(As You Like It
Act IV Scene 1)

Malcolm:
. . .the king-becoming graces,
As justice, verity, temp'rance, stableness,
Bounty, perseverance, mercy, lowliness,
Devotion, patience, courage, fortitude
(Macbeth
Act IV Scene 3)

Diazeugma: [di a ZEUG ma; Greek, *dia,* apart and *zeugnynai,* to join]

The use of one subject with many verbs; the opposite of **zeugma** where one verb is used for many subjects. (See **Zeugma)**

Polonius:
. . .what might you
Or my dear majesty your queen here think,
If I had played the desk or table-book,
Or given my heart a working mute and dumb,
Or looked upon this love with idle sight,
What might you think?
(Hamlet
Act II Scene 2)

Norfolk:
He [the only subject] *bites his lip and starts,*

Steps on a sudden, looks upon the ground,
Then lays his finger on his temple; straight
Springs out into fast gait, then stops again,
Strikes his breast hard, and anon he casts
His eye against the moon.
(Henry VIII
Act III Scene 2)

Ecphonisis: **[ek fo NE sis; Greek, *ekphonein*, to cry out, pronounce]**

Also **exclamatio [Latin, ex, out, and clamare, to cry or shout]**

An outcry to reveal emotions such as wonder, despair, indignation, scorn, grief, misery, etc. Often an **ecphonisis** begins with an O! which the actor must learn to voice fully in order to explore its expressive potential.

Ophelia:
O, what a noble mind is here o'er thrown!
(Hamlet
Act III Scene 1)

Cleopatra:
O, from Italy!
Rain thou thy fruitful tidings in mine ears,
That long time have been barren.
(Antony and Cleopatra
Act II Scene 5)

Leontes:
O, she's warm!
If this be magic, let it be an art
Lawful as eating.

(The Winter's Tale
Act V Scene 3)

King Richard:
Slave, I have set my life upon a cast,
And will stand the hazard of the die.
I think there by six Richmonds in the field;
Five have I slain today instead of him.
A horse! A horse! My kingdom for a horse!
(Richard III
Act V Scene 4)

Elision: **[Latin, *elidere,* to strike off]**

Leaving off the last vowel sound. See more examples in **Part I** above.

Ulysses:
Besides th'applause and approbation. . .
(Troilus and Cressida
Act I Scene 3)

Leontes:
And many a man there is (even at this present,
Now, while I speak this) holds his wife by th'arm.
(*The Winter's Tale*
Act I Scene 2)

Ellipsis: **[e LIP sis; Greek, *elleipsis,* a falling short, omission]**

The omission of expected words, words which are intended to be understood even though they are omitted. (The Greek term is **brachylogy**). The words in parentheses below are left out of the text, but need to be understood if the sentences are to make sense:

Flavius:
No care, no stop! So senseless of expense
That he will neither know how to maintain it,
Nor cease his flow of riot: [he] *takes no*
account
How things go from him, nor resumes no care
Of what is to continue
(Timon of Athens
Act II Scene 2)

Nor dare I question with my jealous thought
Where you may be, or your affairs suppose,
But, like a sad slave, stay and think of naught
Save, where you are how happy you make
those. [who are also there]
So true a fool is love that in your will,
Though you do any thing, he thinks no ill.
(Sonnet #57)

O how shall summers honey breath hold out
Against the wreckful siege of battering days,
When rocks impregnable are not so stout,
Nor gates of steel so strong but time decays?
[them]
(Sonnet #65)

Enallage see Anthimeria

Encomuim: [en KO mi um; Greek, *enkomion,* a hymn in honor of a victor, a song of praise]

The commendation or high praise of a person or thing, particularly extolling inherent qualities. See also **Panagyric.**

Mark Antony:
[Speaking over the body of Brutus]
<u>*This was the noblest Roman of them all*</u>*:*
All the conspirators save only he
Did that they did in envy of great Caesar;
He only, in a general honest thought
And common good to all, made one of them.
His life was gentle, and the elements
So mixed in him that Nature might stand up
Say to all the world 'This was a man.'
(Julius Caesar
Act V Scene 5)

Fortinbras:
Let four captains
<u>*Bear Hamlet like a soldier to the stage,*</u>
<u>*For he was likely, had he been put on,*</u>
<u>*To have proved most royal*</u>*; and for his passage,*
The soldier's music and the rite of war
Speak loudly for him.
(Hamlet
Act V Scene 2)

Portia:
Is it your dear friend that is thus in trouble?

Bassanio:
<u>*The dearest friend to me, the kindest man,*</u>
<u>*The best conditioned and unwearied spirit*</u>
In doing courtesies: <u>*and one in whom*</u>
<u>*The ancient Roman honour more appears*</u>
<u>*Than any that draws breath in Italy.*</u>
(The Merchant of Venice
Act III Scene 2)

Enigma: **[e NIG ma; Greek, *ainigma,* a riddle, dark saying]**

(Puttenham's term: 'the Riddle')

A figurer of deliberate obscurity, where the speaker tries to puzzle the listener. In the example from *Coriolanus* below, Shakespeare names the figure itself, a proof that he used his figures of speech knowingly and not just instinctively.

1 Citizen:
You have deserved nobly of your country, and you have not deserved nobly.

Coriolanus:
Your enigma?

1 Citizen:
You have been a scourge to her enemies; you have been a rod to her friends. You have not indeed lived the common people.
(Coriolanus
Act II Scene 3)

Fool:
Let go thy hold when a great wheel runs down a hill, lest it break thy neck with following; but the great one that goes upward, let him draw thee after. When a wise man gives thee better counsel, give me mine again. I would ha' none but knaves use it, since a fool gives it. That sir which serves and seeks for gain
And follows but for form,
Will pack when it begins to rain
And leave thee in the storm.
But I will tarry; the Fool will stay
And let the wise man fly.

The knave turns fool that runs away;
Fool no knave, perdy.
(King Lear
Act II Scene 3)

2nd Apparition:
Macbeth! Macbeth! Macbeth!

Macbeth:
Had I three ears, I'ld hear thee.

2nd Apparation
Be bloody, bold, and resolute: laugh to scorn
The power of man; for none of woman born
Shall harm Macbeth.

Macbeth:
Then live, Macduff: what need I fear of thee?
(Macbeth
Act IV Scene 1)

Enjambement: [en JAM ment; French, *enjamber,* to encroach, from *en*, in, and *jambe*, leg]

One line of verse running over at the end into the next one. As Shakespeare's style matured he used **enjambment** more and end-stopped lines less. When **enjambment** is at work, actors need to stress the last word of the first line and the first important word of the next line in order to sustain the verse and to communicate the dramatic push forward of the character's ideas and emotions.

Th'expense of spirit in a waste of shame
Is lust in action, and till action, lust
Is perjured, murd'rous, bloody, full of blame
(Sonnet #129)

Macbeth:
Time, thou anticipat'st my dread exploits:
The flighty purpose never is o'ertook
Unless the deed go with it. From this moment
The very firstlings of my heart shall be
The firstlings of my hand.
(Macbeth
Act IV Scene 1)

Hotspur:
Let each man do his best. And here draw I
A sword, whose temper I intend to stain
With the best blood that I can meet withal
In the adventure of this perilous day.
(Henry IV Part I
Act V Scene 2)

Enumeratio: [e nu mer A tio; Latin, *enumerare,* to count over, from *e-*, out, and *numerare*]

Also called **aparithmesis and eutrepismus..** Enumerating for emphasis. Touchstone uses this figure twice in the dialogue below, first in a list, then in another list, enumerated.

Jaques:
He hath been a courtier, he swears.

Touchstone:
If any man doubt that, let him put me to my purgation. I have trod a measure – I have flattered a lady—I have been politic with my friend, smooth with mine enemy—I have undone three tailors—I have had four quarrels, and like to have fought one.

Jaques:

And how was that ta'en up?

Touchstone:
Faith, we met, and found the quarrel was upon the seventh cause. . .

Jaques:
How did you find the quarrel on the seventh cause?

Touchstone:
Upon a lie seven times removed . . . bear your body more seeming, Audrey. . . I will name you the degrees. The first, the Retort Courteous; the second, the Quip Modest; the third, the Reply Churlish; the fourth, the Reproof Valiant; the fifth, the Countercheck Quarrelsome; the sixth, the Lie with Circumstance; the seventh, the Lie Direct . . All these you may avoid, but the Lie Direct; and you may avoid that too, with an If. I knew when seven justices could not take up a quarrel, but when the parties were met themselves, one of them thought but of an If, as, 'If you said so, then I said so', and they shook hands and swore brothers. Your If is the only peace-maker; much virtue in If.
(As You Like It
Act V Scene 4)

Gremio:
First, as you know, my house within the city
Is richly furnished with plate and gold,
Basins and ewers to lave her dainty hands;
My hangings all of Tyrian tapestry;
In ivory coffers I have stuffed my crowns,
In cypress chests my arras counterpoints,

Costly apparel, tents, and canopies,
Fine linen, Turkey cushions bossed with
pearl,
Valance of Venice gold in needlework,
Pewter and brass, and all things that belong
To house or housekeeping. Then, at my farm
I have a hundred milch-kine to the pail,
Six score fat oxen standing in my stalls,
And all things answerable to this portion.
(The Taming of the Shrew
Act II Scene 1)

In the example below Shakespeare enjoys mocking this figure.

Don Pedro:
Officers, what offence have these men done?

Dogberry:
Marry, sir, they have committed false report—moreover, they have spoken untruths—secondarily, they are slanders—sixth and lastly, they have belied a lady—thirdly, they have verified unjust things—and to conclude, they are lying knaves.

Don Pedro:
First, I ask thee what they have done—thirdly, I ask thee what's their offence—sixth and lastly, why they are committed—and to conclude, what you lay to their charge.

Claudio:
Rightly reasoned, and in his own division; and by my troth there's one meaning and well suited.
(Much Ado About Nothing

Act V Scene 1)

Claudio's "Rightly reasoned, and in his own division" indicates Shakespeare was clearly aware of the use of the figures of division: **eutrepismus** (a kind of division related to **aparithmesis** and **enumeratio**) in particular, which numbers and orders things under consideration.

Epanalepsis: **[e pa na LEP sis; Greek, from *epi,* upon, and *ana,* up or again, and *lepsis,* a taking]**

Ending a clause or sentence with the word that begins it. This results often in **Chiasmus** or **Antimetabole** (see above), and sometimes **Antithesis** – all among Shakespeare's most frequently used figures.

Citizen:
Blood hath bought blood, and blows have answered blows:
Strength matched with strength, and power confronted power.
(King John
Act II Scene 1)

Lear:
Nothing will come of nothing.
(King Lear
Act I Scene 1)

Helena:
Weigh oath with oath and you will nothing weigh.
(A Midsummer Night's Dream
Act III Scene 2)

Pistol:
To suck, to suck, the very blood to suck.
(Henry V
Act II Scene 3)

Coriolanus:
Purpose so barr'd, it follows
Nothing is done to purpose.
(Coriolanus
Act III Scene 1)

Cassius:
Cassius from bondage will deliver Cassius.
(Julius Caesar
Act I Scene 3)

Brutus:
Remember March, the ides of March
remember.
(Julius Caesar
Act IV Scene 3)

Epanorthosis: or correctio [e pan or THO sis; Greek, *epi*, upon and *arorthoun*, to set]

Amending or correcting an initial statement in order to make it more vehement, stronger.

King Henry:
A good heart, Kate, is the sun and the moon;
or rather the sun and not the moon, for it
shines bright and never changes, but keeps
Its course truly.
(Henry V
Act V Scene 2)

Adam:

Your brother (no, no brother!) Yet the son –
(Yet not the son – I will not call him son)
Of him I was about to call his father
Hath heart your praises, and this night he means
To burn the lodging where you use to lie
And you within it.
(As You Like It
Act II Scene 3)

(Note the use of **aposiopesis** in the above speech)

Petruchio:
They shall go forward, Kate, at thy command.
Obey the bride, you that attend on her!
Go to the feast, revel and domineer,
Carouse full measure to her maidenhead,
Be mad and merry, or go hang yourselves;
But for my bonny Kate, she must with me.
Nay, look not big, nor stamp, nor stare, nor fret,
I will be master of what is my own.
She is my goods, my chattels; she is my house,
My household stuff, my field, my barn,
My horse, my ox, my ass, my any thing –
And here she stands, touch her whoever dare!
I'll bring my action on the proudest he
That stops my way in Padua. Grumio,
Draw forth thy weapon, we are beset with thieves,
Rescue thy mistress, if thou be a man.
Fear not, sweet wench, they shall not touch thee, Kate!
I'll buckler thee against a million.
(The Taming of the Shrew
Act III Scene 2)

Epimone: **[e PI mo ne; Greek, tarrying or delay]**

(Puttenham's term: 'the Loveburden')

The repeated final phrase of a song.

Desdemona:
The poor soul sat sighing by a sycamore tree,
Sing all a green willow;
Her hand on her bosom, her head on her knee,
Sing willow, willow, willow:
The fresh streams ran by her and murmured her moans;
Sing willow, willow, willow;
Her salt tears fell from her, and softened the stones –

Lay by these –
Sing willow, willow, willow.
(Othello Act IV Scene 3)

Feste:
When that I was and a little tiny boy,
With hey, ho, the wind and the rain:
A foolish thing was but a toy ,
For the rain it raineth every day.

But when I came to man's estate
With hey, ho, the wind and the rain:
'gainst knaves and thieves men shut their gate,
For the rain it raineth every day.

But when I came alas to wive,

With hey, ho, the wind and the rain:
By swaggering could I never thrive,
For the rain it raineth every day.
(Twelfth Night
Act V Scene 1)

Epistrophe: [e PIS tro fe; Greek, turning about from, *epistrephein*, to turn about]

Using the same word at the end of successive phrases. Lapham also calls this by its rhetorical (as opposed to grammatical) name **antistrophe**.

Anne:
Thou wast the cause of that accursed effect.

Richard:
Your beauty was the cause of that effect.
(Richard III
Act I Scene 2)

This hand. which for thy love did kill thy love
Shall, for thy love, kill a far truer love.
(Richard III
Act I Scene 2)

Macbeth:
And if we fail?

Lady Macbeth:
We fail.
But screw your courage to the sticking place
And we'll not fail.
(Macbeth
Act I, Scene 7)

Demetrius:
I love thee not, therefore pursue me not. . .
Thou told'st me they were stol'n into this
wood;
And here am I, and wood within this wood . .

(A Midsummer Night's Dream
Act III, Scene 2)

Epitheton: **[e PI the ton; Greek, *epitithena*, to put on]**

(Puttenham's term: 'the Qualifier' or 'the figure of Attribution')

Naming something and adding a descriptive quality to it; to qualify something by adding an attribution. See **Epithet, Part I.**

Prospero:
Why that's my dainty Ariel.
(The Tempest
Act V Scene 1)

Armado:
Tender juvenal!
(Love's Labour's Lost
Act I Scene 2)

Troilus:
Your leave, sweet Cressid?
(Troilus and Cressida
Act III Scene 2)

Pistol:
Bardolph, a soldier firm and sound of heart
And of buxom valour hath, by cruel fate,
And giddy Fortune's furious fickle wheel,

That goddess blind,
That stands upon the rolling restless stone

--

Fluellen:
By your patience, Ancient Pistol . . .
(Henry V
Act III Scene 6)

Sister Miriam Joseph notes (*SUAL* p124) "The compound epithet, although not mentioned by the Tudor rhetoricians in their treatment of **epitheton**,was popular with Elizabethan writers and merits consideration here because Shakespeare used it more copiously and with greater freedom than his fellow dramatists, and by means of it created language picturesque, sudden, and evocative." Her examples include:

Cleopatra:
Now from head to foot
I am marble-constant.
(Antony and Cleopatra
Act V Scene 2)

Thersites:
Thou mongrel beef-witted lord.
(Troilus and Cressida
Act II Scene 1)

Jupiter:
How dare you ghosts
Accuse the thunderer, whose bolt, you know,
Sky-planted batters all rebelling coasts.
(Cymbeline
Act V Scene 4)

Epizeuxis: **[ep i ZEUX is; Greek, *epizeuxis*, a joining together]**

(Puttenham's term: 'the Underlay or Coocko-spel')

A phrase or word repeated without interruption, for emphasis.

Macduff:
Oh, horror, horror, horror.
(Macbeth
Act II Scene 3)

Lear:
And when we have stol'n upon these son-in-laws,
Then kill, kill, kill, kill, kill, kill!
(King Lear
Act IV, Scene 6)

Bottom:
Then die, die, die, die, die.
(A Midsummer Night's Dream
Act V)

Helena:
Is't not enougn is't not enough, young man?
(A Midsummer Night's Dream
Act III Scene 2)

Pandarus:
Asses, fools, dolts; chaff and bran, chaff and bran; porridge after meat. I could live and die in the eyes of Troilus. Ne'er look, ne'er look. The eagles are gone; crows and daws, crows and daws.
(Troilus and Cressida
Act I Scene 2)

Eponym: **[E po nym; Greek, *eponymos,* given as a name; *epi*, upon, and *onyma*, a name]**

A name suited to the nature of the character. Compared to other writers (Ben Jonson, for instance, or Richard Sheridan a hundred and sixty years later) Shakespeare used this technique sparingly rather than continuously:

Puck, Bottom, Flute, Snout, Snug, Starveling
(A Midsummer Night's Dream)

Sir Toby Belch, Andrew Aguecheek, Malvolio
(Twelfth Night)

Moldy, Shadow, Wart, Feeble, Bullcalf;
Doll Tearsheet
(Henry IV Part 2)

Pandarus
(Troilus and Cressida)

Etiologia: or **aetiologia [ay ti o LO gia; Greek, *aitologia,* from *aitia*, cause, and *logia,* description]**

(Puttenham's term: 'the Reason Rend' or 'the Tell Cause')

To give a reason or cause for a thought or an action.

Hamlet:
Let them be well us'd; <u>for they are the abstract and brief chronicles</u> <u>of the time</u>.
(Hamlet
Act II Scene 2)

Cleopatra:

I will employ thee back again; I find thee
Most fit for business.
(Antony and Cleopatra
Act III Scene 4)

Paris:
Younger than she are happy mothers made.

Capulet:
And too soon marred are those so early made.
Earth hath swallowed all my hopes but she;
She is the hopeful lady of my earth.
(Romeo and Juliet
Act I Scene 2)

Eulogia: **[yu LO gia; Greek, *eulogia,* speaking praise, blessing]**

Sometimes conflated with **encomium** above, but **eulogia** more particularly refers to the pronouncing of a blessing:

Hyman:
Here's eight that must take hands,
To join in Hyman's bands,
If truth holds true contents.
You and you no cross shall part:
You and you are heart in heart:
You to his love must accord,
Or have a woman to your lord.
You and you are sure together,
As the winter to foul weather.
Whiles a wedlock-hymn we sing,
Feed yourselves with questioning;
That reason wonder may diminish
How thus we met, and these things finish.
(As You Like It

Act V Scene 4)

Horatio:
Good night, sweet Prince.
And <u>flights of angels sing thee to thy rest</u>.
(Hamlet
Act V Scene 2)

Brutus:
<u>The last of all the Romans, fare thee well</u>!
It is impossible that ever Rome
Should breed thy fellow. Friends, I owe mo tears
To this dead man than you shall see me pay.
<u>I shall find time, Cassius, I shall find time</u>.
(Julius Caesar
Act V Scene 4)

Oberon:
Now, until the break of day,
Through this house each fairy stray.
To the best bride-bed will we:
Which by us shall blessed be;
And the issue, there create
Ever shall be fortunate:
So shall all the couples three
Ever true in loving be:
And the blots of Nature's hand
Shall not in their issue stand. . . .
Every fairy take his gait,
<u>And each several chamber bless</u>
<u>Through this palace, with sweet peace</u>;
<u>And the owner of it blest</u>
<u>Ever shall in safety rest</u>.
Trip away. Make no stay:
Meet me all by break of day.
(A Midsummer Night's Dream

Act V Scene 1)

Eutrepismus: **[yu tre PIS mus; Greek, numbering and ordering parts under consideration. See Enumeratio.**

Exclamatio: **[ex cla MA tio; Latin, *exclamatio,* calling or crying out]**

See **Ecphonisis.**

Exuscitatio: **[ex u si TA tio; Latin, *exsuscita*, *ex* plus *suscitare*, to rouse, to rouse up, wake out of sleep]**

Expressing acute feeling in order to inspire the hearer to feel the same profound emotion.

Juliet:
Come weep with me-- past hope, pasts cure,
past help!
(Romeo and Juliet
Act IV Scene 1)

Hermia:
What? Can you do me greater harm than
hate?
Hate me! Wherefore? O me, what news, my
love?
Am not I Hermia? Are you not Lysander?
I am as fair now as I was erewhile.
Since night you loved me . . .
(A Midsummer Night's Dream
Act III Scene 2)

(Note: the lovers' quarrel – the great Scene 2 of Act III in *A Midsummer Night's Dream* -- is a brilliant set of variations on, the figure of **exuscitatio**. The scene below between Hubert and Arthur is also built around e**xuscitatio**).

Arthur:
Must you with hot irons, burn out both mine eyes?

Hubert:
Young boy, I must.

Arthur:
And will you?

Hubert:
And I will.

Arthur:
Have you the heart? When your head did but ache,
I knit my handkercher about your brow. . .

O, save me, Hubert, save me! my eyes are out,
Even with the fierce look of these bloody men.
Alas, what need you be so boist'rous rough?
I will not struggle, I will stand stone-still:
For heaven's sake, Hubert, let me not be bound!
Nay, hear me, Hubert, drive these men away,
And I will sit a quiet as a lamb.
(King John
Act IV Scene 1)

Hendiadys: **[hen DY a dis; Greek, *hen dia dyoin,* one by two]**

(Puttenham's term: 'Endiadis: the Figure of Twinnes')

A figure of speech where two nouns connected by 'and' are used instead of one noun or a noun and an adjective. See the masterful analysis of the use of **hendiadys** in *Hamlet*, pp321, 322 in *1599, a Year in the Life of William Shakespeare* by James Shapiro.

Puck:
Take heed the queen come not within his sight;
For Oberon is passing fell and wrath. . .
(A Midsummer Night's Dream
Act I, Scene 1)

Titania:
And this same progeny of evils comes
From our debate, from our dissension;
We are their parents and original.
(A Midsummer Night's Dream
Act II, Scene 1)

Hamlet:
Angels and ministers of grace defend us.
(Hamlet
Act I, Scene 4)

Hamlet:
They are the abstract and brief chronicles of the time.
(Hamlet
Act II, Scene 2)

Hamlet:
Had he the motive and the cue for passion –
(Hamlet
Act II, Scene 2)

Hamlet:
Fit and seasoned for his passage.
(Hamlet
Act III, Scene 3)

Hamlet:
If damned custom have not brassed it so
That it be proof and bulwark against sense.
(Hamlet
Act III, Scene 4)

Hamlet:
The book and volume of my brain.
(Hamlet
Act I, Scene 5)

Hamlet:
A fantasy and a trick of fame
(Hamlet
Act IV, Scene 4)

Macbeth:
Full of sound and fury. . .
(Macbeth
Act V, Scene 5)

Hirmus: See **Irmus**

Homiologia: **[hom I o LO gia; Greek, uniformity of style, *homio* and *logia*, word] See also Tautologia**

"when the whole matter is all alike, and hath no varietie to avoyde tediousness" (Sherry quoted by Sister Miriam Joseph, SUAL, p302)

Tedious, redundant style. Needless and inane repetition. Used by Shakespeare to create humorous characterizations.

Shallow:
He hath wrong'd me; indeed he hath; at a word, he hath. Believe me! Robert Shallow, Esquire, saith he is wronged.

(The Merry Wives of Windsor Act I Scene 1)

Shallow:
I will not excuse you; you shall not be excus'd; excuses shall not be admitted, there is no excuse shall serve; you shall not be excus'd.

(Henry IV Part II Act V Scene 1)

Bottom:
Nay, you must name his name, and half his face must be seen through the lion's neck, and he himself must speak through, saying thus, or to the same defect: 'Ladies,' or 'Fair ladies—I would wish you,' or 'I would request you,' or 'I would entreat you, not to fear, not to tremble: my life for yours. If you think I come hither as a lion it were pity of my life. No, I am no such thing: I am a man as other men are.' And there indeed let him name his name, and tell them plainly he is Snug the joiner.

(A Midsummer Night's Dream Act III Scene 1)

Homoioteleuton: **[hom oi o te LEU ton; Greek, *homos*, like, *teleuton*, ending]**

Like endings: a series of words ending alike;

Julia:

How churlishly I chid Lucetta hence
When willingly I would have had her here!
How angerly I taught my brow to frown . . .
(The Two Gentlemen of Verona
Act I Scene 2)

Farewell! Thou art too dear for my
possessing . . .
For how do I hold thee but by thy granting.
And for that riches where is my deserving?
The cause of this fair gift in me is wanting
And so my patent back again is swerving.
Thy self thou gav'st, thy own worth then not
knowing,
Or me to whom thou gave'st it, else mistaking,
So thy great gift upon misprision growing,
Comes home again, on better judgment
making.
(Sonnet #87)

Rhymed endings are a kind of **homoioteleuton.** Lanham discusses this term in detail (HRT, p540).

Hypallage: **[hy PAL la ge; Greek, *hypallage*, an exchange or interchange from *hypo,* under and *allassein,* to change]**

(Puttenham's term: 'the changeling')

A kind of **hyperbaton** where words are applied in an unexpected, sometimes absurd way. As is often the case, Shakespeare used peculiar linguistic devices to create comedic characters. Whereas Dogberry in *Much Ado About Nothing* is characterized by **catachresis** (an understandable confusion of like words confused with each other) Bottom in *A Midsummer Night's Dream* is characterized by **hypallage.**

Bottom:
The eye of man hath not heard, the ear of man hath not seen, man's hand is not able to taste, his tongue to conceive, nor his heart to report what my dream was.
(A Midsummer Night's Dream
Act IV Scene 1)

Bottom:
I see a voice. Now will I to the chink,
To spy an I can hear my Thisby's face.

Bottom:
Will it please you see the Epilogue, or to hear a Bergomask dance between two of our company?
(A Midsummer Night's Dream
Act V Scene 1)

Hyperbaton: [hy PER ba ton; Greek, *hyberbatos,* from *hyperbainein*, to step over]

The transposition or rearrangement of usual sentence order.

Richard:
Draw near,
And list what with our council we have done.
(Richard II
Act I Scene 3)

Him in thy course untainted do allow
For beauty's pattern to succeeding men.
Yet, do thy worst, old Time: despite thy wrong,

My love shall in my verse ever live young.
(Sonnet #19)

<u>A woman's face with Nature's own hand</u>
<u>painted</u>
<u>Hast thou, the master-mistress of my passion</u>;
A woman's gentle heart, but not acquainted
With shifting change, as is false women's
fashion. . .
And for a woman wert thou first created,
Till Nature as she wrought thee fell a-doting,
And by addition me of thee defeated,
By adding one thing to my purpose nothing.
But since she pricked thee out for women's
pleasure,
Mine be thy love, and thy love's use their
treasure.
(Sonnet #20)

But out, alack! he was but one hour mine;
The region cloud hath mask'd him from me
now.
<u>Yet him for this my love no whit disdaineth</u>;
Sons of the world may stain when heaven's
sun staineth.
(Sonnet #33)

<u>From you have I been absent in the spring</u>,
When proud-pied April dress'd in all his trim
Hath put a spirit of youth in every thing,
That heavy Saturn laugh'd and leap'd with
him.
Yet nor the lays of birds nor the sweet smell
Of different flowers in odour and in hue
Could make me any summer's story tell,
Or from their proud lap pluck them where
they grew;

Nor did I wonder at the lily's white,
Nor praise the deep vermilion in the rose;
They were but sweet, but figures of delight,
Drawn after you, you pattern of all those.
Yet seem'd it winter still, and, you away,
As with your shadow I with these did play.
(Sonnet #98)

Hyperbole: **[hy PER bo le; Greek, from *hyper*, over or beyond, and *ballein*, to throw]**

(Puttenham's term: 'the Over Reacher' or 'the Loud Lyer')

Excessive or extravagant terms used in description, not intended to be taken literally. The use of **hyperbole** is filled with energy and lifts many of Shakespeare's characters and situations above the ordinary. See further examples in **Part I**.

Petruchio:
Think you a little din can daunt mine ears?
Have I not in my time heard lions roar?
Have I not heard the sea, puffed up with winds
Rage like an angry boar chafed with sweat?
Have I not heard great ordnance in the field
And heaven's artillery thunder in the skies?
Have I not in a pitched battle heard
Loud 'larums, neighing steeds, and trumpets clang?
And do you tell me of a woman's tongue
That gives not half so great a blow to hear
As will a chestnut in a farmer's fire?
Tush, tush, fear boys with bugs.
(The Taming of the Shrew Act I scene 2)

Cleopatra:
His face was as the heav'ns, and therein stuck
A sun and moon, which kept their course and
lighted
The little O, the earth. . . .
His legs bestrid the ocean: his rear'd arm
Crested the world . . . Realms and islands
were
As plates dropp'd from his pocket.
(Antony and Cleopatra
Act II Scene 2)

Troilus:
He brought a Grecian queen, whose youth
and freshness
Wrinkles Apollo's and makes stale the
morning.
(Troilus and Cressida
Act II Scene 2)

Hypercatalectic or Hypermetrical:[HY per ka ta LEK tik; Greek, *hyper,* beyond, and *katalekticos,* stopping off, incomplete]

An iambic pentameter verse line containing an extra or eleventh syllable at the end; commonly referred to as a line with a feminine ending. For more examples see **Part I, Iambic Pentameter**.

Hamlet:
To be or not to be, that is the ques<u>tion</u>. . .
(Hamlet
Act III Scene 1)

Farewell! Thou art to dear for my posses<u>sing</u>.

(Sonnet #87)

Katharine:
I am ashamed that women are so simple. . .
(The Taming of the Shrew
Act V Scene 2)

Hypermonosyllable: [HY per MA no si la bl; Greek, *hyper,* beyond, *mono,* one]

The contracting of a two syllable word (usually with a weak, non-plosive internal consonant) into one syllable, i.e. *pow'r* for *power*, *flow'r* for *flower.* Shakespeare does this frequently as it gives him flexibility of rhythm. Furthermore, names like Troilus or words like ocean are scanned as three syllables (*Troy-eh-lus, o-ce-an*) or two syllables (*Troi-lus*, *o-cean*) depending on the number of syllables needed in the rhythm of the line. For examples, see **Apocope** and **Syncope**)

Hypotyposis: [HY po ty PO sis; Greek, *hypo,* under, *typos,* figure or image]

Exceptionally vivid description for the dramatic and rhetorical effect of making listeners see what is described as dramatically as if they were there. For a related figure see **Hyperbole** above.

Macbeth:
Come, seeling night,
Scarf up the tender eye of pitiful day,
And with thy bloody and invisible hand
Cancel and tear to pieces that great bond
Which keeps me paled! Light thickens, and the crow
Makes wing to th' rooky wood:

Good things of day begin to droop and
drowse,
Whiles night's black agents to their preys do
rouse.
(Macbeth
Act III Scene 2)

Edgar:
Come on, sir, here's the place: stand still;
how fearful
And dizzy 'tis to cast one's eyes so low!
The crows and choughs that wing the midway
air
Show scarce so gross as beetles. Half way
down
Hangs one that gathers samphire—dreadful
trade!
Methinks he seems no bigger than his head.
The fishermen that walk upon the beach
Appear like mice: and yond tall and
anchoring bark
Diminished to her cock; her cock a buoy
Almost too small for sight. The murmuring
surge,
That on th'unnumb'red idle pebble chafes,
Cannot be heard so high. I'll look no more,
Lest my brain turn, and the deficient sight
Topple down headlong.
(King Lear
Act IV Scene 5)

Enobarbus:
The barge she sat in, like a burnisht throne
Burned on the water: the poop was beaten
gold;
Purple the sails, and so perfumed that
The winds were love-sick with them; the oars

were silver,
Which to the tune of flutes kept stroke and made
The water which they beat to follow faster,
As amorous of their strokes. For her own person,
It beggared all description, she did lie
In her pavilion, cloth-of-gold, of tissue,
O'er picturing that Venus where we see
The fancy outwork nature: on each side her
Stood pretty dimpled boys, like smiling Cupids,
With divers-coloured fans, whose wind did seem
To glow the delicate cheeks which they did cool,
And what they undid did.

(Antony and Cleopatra Act II Scene 2)

Hypozeuxis: [hy po ZEUX is; Greek, *hypo,* under]

When every phrase in a complex sentence is complete with repetition of a subject and a verb each time. Compare with **diazeugma** where one subject works for many verbs, and **zeugma** where one verb serves multiple subjects. **Hypozeuxis** often produces **isocolon** (a sequence of phrases of the same structure) (See **Diazeugma, Zeugma, and Isocolon)**

Launce:
I think Crab, my dog, be the sourest-natured dog that lives: <u>my mother weeping</u>; <u>my father wailing</u>; <u>my sister crying</u>; <u>our maid howling</u>; <u>our cat wringing her hands</u>; <u>and all our house in a great perplexity</u>.

(The Two Gentlemen of Verona

Act II Scene 1)

Servingman:
Madam, the guests are come, supper serv'd up, you call'd, my young lady ask'd for, the nurse curs'd in the pantry, and everything in extremity.
(Romeo and Juliet
Act I Scene 3)

Berowne:
What, I? I love? I sue? I seek a wife?
(Love's Labour's Lost
Act III Scene 1)

Hysteron Proteron: [HIS te ron PRO te ron; Greek, from *hysteron*, latter, and *proteron*, former]

A kind of **hyperbaton** which involves reversing the order of happenings in a sentence so that which would normally come first goes last.

Dogberry:
Masters, it is proved already that you are little better than false knaves, and it will go near to be thought so shortly.
(Much Ado About Nothing
Act IV Scene 2)

Enobarbus:
Naught, naught, all naught! I can behold no longer:
Th'Antoniad, the Egyptian admiral,
With all their sixty, fly and turn the rudder:
To see 't myne eyes are blasted.
(Antony and Cleopatra
Act III Scene 10)

Othello:
Yet I'll not shed her blood;
Nor scar that whiter skin of hers than snow.
(Othello
Act V Scene 2)

Insultatio: **[in sul TA ti o; Latin, *insultare,* to leap upon]**

Deriding or abusing a person to his face. Shakespeare's skill at inventive insults is recognized even today with popular games and collections based on them.

Antonio:
Content yourself, God knows I loved my niece,
And she is dead, slandered to death by
villains,
That dare as well answer a man indeed
As I dare take a serpent by the tongue.
Boys, apes, braggarts, Jacks, milksops. . . .
Scambling, out-facing, fashion-monging boys,
That lie, and cog, and flout, deprave, and
slander,
Go anticly, and show outward hideousness,
And speak off half a dozen dang'rous words,
How they might hurt their enemies, if they
durst. . .
(Much Ado About Nothing
Act V Scene 1)

Queen Margaret:
From forth the kennel of thy womb hath crept
A hell-hound that doth hunt us all to death:
That dog, that had his teeth before his eyes,

To worry lambs and lap their gentle blood;
That foul defacer of God's handiwork;
That excellent grand tyrant of the earth,
That reigns in galled eyes of weeping souls –
Thy womb let loose, to chase us to our graves.
(Richard III
Act IV Scene 4)

Macbeth:
The devil damn thee black, thou cream-faced loon!
(Macbeth
Act V Scene 3)

L. Chief Justice:
Do you set down your name in the scroll of youth, that are written down old with all the characters of age? Have you not a moist eye? A dry hand? a yellow cheek? a white beard? a decreasing leg? an increasing belly? is not your voice broken? your wind short? your chin double? your wit single? and every part of you blasted with antiquity? and will you call yourself young? Fie, fie, fie, Sir John!
(Henry IV Part 2
Act I Scene 2)

Inter se pugnantia: [IN ter se pug NAN ti a; Latin, *inter se*, between, among themselves *pugnantia*, of opponants]

Pointing out to an opponent's face his hypocrisy; by extension, a struggle between theory and practice. Since internal conflict plays such a large role in Shakespearean characters this is a frequently used figure in **soliloquies** when a character questions the morality of his own actions.

Ophelia:
But, good my brother,
Do not as some ungracious pastors do,
Show me the steep and thorny way to heaven,
Whiles, like a puff'd and reckless libertine,
Himself the primrose path of dalliance treads
And recks not his own rede.
(Hamlet
Act I Scene 3)

Portia:
It is a good divine that follows his own instructions. I can easier teach twenty what were good to be done than be one of the twenty to follow mine own teaching.
(The Merchant of Venice
Act I Scene 2)

Juliet:
Thou knowest the mask of night is on my face;
Else would a maiden blush bepaint my cheek,
For that which thou hast heard me speak tonight.
Fain would I dwell on form; fain, fain deny
What I have spoke: but farewell compliment!
Dost thou love me? I know thou wilt say 'Ay',
And I will take thy word. Yet, if thou swear'st,
Thou may'st prove false. At lovers' perjuries
They say Jove laughs. O gentle Romeo,
If thou dost love, pronounce it faithfully.
Or if thou think'st I am too quickly won,
I'll frown and be perverse and say thee nay,
So thou wilt woo; but else, not for the world.
(Romeo and Juliet
Act II Scene 1)

Macbeth:
I am settled, and bend up
Each corporal agent to this terrible feat.
Away and mock the time with fairest show:
False face must hide what the false heart doth know.
(Macbeth
Act I Scene 7)

Cleopatra:
Know, sir, that I
Will not wait pinioned at your master's court,
Nor once be chastised with the sober eye
Of dull Octavia. Shall they hoist me up
And show me to the shouting varletry
Of censuring Rome? Rather a ditch in Egypt
Be gentle grave unto me! rather on Nilus' mud
Lay me stark nak'd, and let the water-flies
Blow me into abhorring! Rather make
My country's high pyramides my gibbet,
And hang me up in chains--
(Antony and Cleopatra
Act V Scene 2)

Irmus also spelled Hirmus: [IR mus; Greek, *eirein*, to fasten together, join]

(Puttenham's term: 'the Long Loose')

Putting off naming what you're speaking of until the last few words: "**which concludes the whole premises with a perfect sense and full periode**." **(Puttenham) Irmus** is often used in conjunction with **orcos,** the swearing of an oath, to increase the importance of what is being sworn too. See **Orcos** below.

Timon:
Tell my friends,
Tell Athens, in the sequence of degree
From high to low throughout, that whoso please
To stop affliction, let him take his haste,
Come hither ere my tree hath felt the axe,
And hang himself.
(Timon of Athens
Act V Scene 1)

Orlando:
But whate'er you are
That in this desert inaccessible,
Under the shade of melancholy boughs,
Lose and neglect the creeping hours of time;
If ever you have looked on better days;
If ever been where bells have knolled to church;
If ever sat at any good man's feast;
If ever from your eyelids wiped a tear,
And know what 'tis to pity and be pitied,
Let gentleness my strong enforcement be:
In the which hope I blush and hide my sword.
(As You Like It
Act II Scene 7)

Beatrice:
Princes and counties! Surely a princely testimony, a goodly count, Count Comfect – a sweet gallant surely. O that I were a man for his sake! Or that I had any friend that would be a man for my sake! but manhood is melted into curtsies, valour into complement, and

men are only turned into tongue, and trim ones too: he is now as valiant as Hercules, that only tells a lie and swears it . . . I cannot be a man with wishing, therefore I will die a woman with grieving.

(Much Ado About Nothing
Act IV Scene 1)

Lysander:
Ay, by my life!
And never did desire to see thee more.
Therefore be out of hope, of question or doubt:
Be certain, nothing truer; 'tis no jest
That I do hate thee and love Helena.
(A Midsummer Night's Dream
(Act III Scene 2)

Ironia: **[i RO ni a; Greek, *eironeia*, dissimulation]**

(Puttenham's term: 'the Drie Mock') See **Irony** in **Part I** above.

Richard:
Simple, plain Clarence! I do love thee so
That I will shortly send thy soul to heaven,
If heaven will take the present at our hands.
(Richard III
Act I Scene 1)

2 Apparition:
Be bloody, bold, and resolute: laugh to scorn
The power of man, for none of woman born
Shall harm Macbeth.
(Macbeth
Act IV Scene 1)

Richard:
Cousin of Buckingham, and sage, grave men,
Since you will buckle fortune on my back,
To bear her burthen, whe'er I will or no,
I must have patience to endure the load:
But if black scandal or foul-faced reproach
Attend the sequel of your imposition,
Your mere enforcement shall acquittance of
me
From all the impure blots and stains thereof;
For God doth know, and you may partly see,
How far I am from the desire of this.
(Richard III
Act III Scene 7)

Isocolon: **[I so KO lon; Greek, *iso,* equal plus *kolon*, limb]**

Equal lengths of clauses or sentences in sequence. When the sequence is three the figure is a **tricolon.** (See **Tricolon**). The first Shylock example below demonstrates **isocolon** then **tricolon.**

Warwick:
Alas! how should you govern any kingdom,
That know not how to use ambassadors,
Nor how to be contented with one wife,
Nor how to use your brothers brotherly,
Nor how to study for the people's welfare,
Nor how to shroud yourself from enemies?
(Henry VI Part 3
Act 4 Scene 3)

Shylock:

I will buy with you, sell with you, talk with you, walk with you, and so following: but I will not eat with you, drink with you, nor pray with you.

(The Merchant of Venice
Act I Scene 3)

Shylock:
He hath disgraced me and hindred me half a million, laughed at my losses, mocked at my gains, scorned my nation, thwarted my bargains, cooled my friends, heated mine enemies -- and what is his reason? I am a Jew.

(Merchant of Venice
Act 3 Scene 1)

Hermia:
I swear to thee by Cupid's strongest bow,
By his best arrow with the golden head,
By the simplicity of Venus' doves
By that which knitteth souls and prospers loves . . .

(A Midsummer Night's Dream
Act I Scene 1)

Litotes:[LIT o tes; Greek, *litotes,* from *litos,* smooth, plain, small, meager]

(Puttenham's term: 'the Moderator')

A figure of negation in which one denies the contrary; it is often a kind of understatement that intensifies.

Shakespeare loved to use **litotes,** indicated by the many words he employed beginning with 'dis-' and 'un-'. **Litotes** involves a denial of the contrary to the subject. Sister Miriam Joseph notes that this may be used to avoid the appearance of boasting or to veil a threat.(*SUAL* p135). It also can be used to introduce a topic too painful to address directly, or to intensify an intention, as in Gloucester's statement below.

Gloucester:

Let him fly far,
<u>Not in this land shall he remain uncaught.</u>
(King Lear
Act II Scene 1)

Flavius:

I did endure
<u>Not seldom, nor no slight checks, when I have</u>
Prompted you in the ebb of your estate
And your great flow of debts.
(Timon of Athens
Act II Scene 2)

In her introduction to Sister Miriam Joseph's *The Trivium,* Marguerite McGlinn observes (pviii) "he (Shakespeare) often used **litotes**, the figure of speech based on the obversion of a proposition. *The Tempest* shows one instance of this. Sebastian, expressing his concern over the fate of Ferdinand, the king's son, says *'<u>I have no hope that he's undrowned.</u>'* Shakespeare makes the rhetorical decision to use obversion to dramatize that Sebastian faces a reality he cannot describe in direct speech."

Meiosis: **[mei O sis; Greek, from *meioun*, to make smaller]**

(Puttenham's term: 'the Disabler') According to Puttenham, **"To diminish or abase a thing by way of spite or malice.**" Also: ". . .**sometimes for**

modesty's sake, and to avoide the opinion of arrogancy, speaking of ourselves or of others."

Sister Miriam Joseph suggests **meiosis** is the use of euphemism to diminish a fault, such as calling robbery pilfering, or a serious wound just a scratch. The opposite is **paradiastole, w**here one flatters or soothes by suggesting a notorious miser is just thrifty, or avarice just good management. (SUAL,331)

Romeo:
Courage, man; the hurt cannot be much.

Mercutio:
No, 'tis not so deep as a well, nor so wide as a church door, but 'tis enough, 'twill serve.
(Romeo and Juliet
Act III Scene 1)

Marulles:
You blocks, you stones, you worse than senseless things!
(Julius Caesar
Act I Scene 1)

Marcius:
All the contagion of the south light on you,
You shames of Rome!. .
You souls of geese
That bear the shapes of men. . . .
(Coriolanus
Act I Scene 5)

Lysander:
Out, tawny Tartar, out!
Out, loathed medicine! O hated potion, hence!
(A Midsummer Night's Dream
Act III scene 2)

Hermia:
'Puppet'! Why, so? Ay, that way goes the game!
Now I perceive that she hath made compare
Between our statures; she hath urg'd her height;
And with her personage, her tall personage,
Her height, forsooth, she hath prevail'd with him,
And are you grown so high in his esteem
Because I am so dwarfish and so low?
How low am I, thou painted maypole? Speak:
How low am I? I am not yet so low
But that my nails can reach unto thine eyes.
(A Midsummer Night's Dream Act III scene 2)

Helena:
O, when she is angry, she is keen and shrewd;
She was a vixen when she went to school
And though she be but little she is fierce.
(A Midsummer Night's Dream Act III scene 2)

Merismus: [me RIS mus; Greek, *meris*, a part or portion]

Dividing a thing into its parts; also called **partitio;** see also **Aparithmesis, Synonymia** and **Systrophe.**

Caliban:
Then I lov'd thee
And showed thee all the qualities o'th' isle,
The fresh springs, brine-pits, barren place and fertile.
(The Tempest Act I Scene 2)

Lord Chief Justice:
Do you set down your name in the scroll of youth, that are written down old with all the characters of age? Have you not a moist eye, a dry hand, a yellow cheek, a white beard, a decreasing leg, an increasing belly? Is not your voice broken, your wind short, your chin double, your wit single, and every part about you blasted with antiquity? And will you yet call yourself young?
(Henry IV Part 2
Act I Scene 2)

Rosalind:
There is none of my uncle's marks upon you: he taught me how to know a man in love; in which cage of rushes I am sure you are not a prisoner.

Orlando:
What were his marks?

Rosalind:
A lean cheek, which you have not; a blue eye and sunken, which you have not; a beard neglected, which you have not. . . . Then your hose should be ungartered, your bonnet unbanded, your sleeve unbuttoned, your shoe untied, and every thing about you demonstrating a careless desolation.
(As You Like It
Act III Scene 2)

Metalepsis: **[me ta LEP sis; Greek, substitution, from *meta*, among, and *lambanein*, to take]**

(Puttenham's term 'the Farset')

When a far-fetched image is used in place of a simpler one; or when one attributes a present effect to a remote cause. Rosalind criticizes **metalepsis** in claiming a person never dies (present effect) from love (remote cause):

Rosalind:
No, faith, die by attorney: the poor world is almost six thousand years old, and in all this time there was not any man died in his own person, videlicet, in a love cause: Troilus had his brains dashed out with a Grecian club, yet he did what he could to die before, and he is one of the patterns of love: Leander, he would have lived many a fair year, though Hero had turned nun, if it had not been for a hot midsummer night; for, good youth, he went but forth to wash him in the Hellespont and being taken with the cramp was drowned, and the foolish chroniclers of that age found it was 'Hero of Sestos'. But these are all lies. Men have died from time to time, and worms have eaten them, but not for love.
(As You Like It
Act IV Scene 1)

Casca:
Are not you moved, when all the sway of earth
Shapes like a thing unfirm? O Cicero,
I have seen tempests, when the scolding winds
Have rived the knotty oaks, and I have seen
Th'ambitious ocean swell and rage and foam,
To be exalted with the threat'ning clouds;
But never till to-night, never till now,

Did I go through a tempest dropping fire.
Either there is a civil strife in heaven,
Or else the world too saucy with the gods
Incenses them to send destruction.
(Julius Caesar
Act I Scene 3)

Isabella:
There spake my brother! There my father's grave
Did utter forth a voice.
(Measure for Measure
Act III Scene 1)

Metaphora: **[me TA for a; Greek, transference, from *meta,* over, and *pherein*, to bear]**

(Puttenham's term: 'the Figure of Transporte')

A comparative figure where one says something *is* something else.

Gonzalo:
His complexion is a perfect gallows
(The Tempest
Act I Scene 1)

For more examples see **Metaphor** in **Part I.**

Metonymy: **[me TON i mee; Greek, *metonymi,* a change of name, *meta,* denoting change plus *onoma,* name]**

Figure of speech in which an attribute or commonly associated feature of something is used to name or designate the whole.

King Henry:
So minutes, hours, days, months, and years,

Pass'd over to the end they were created,
Would bring <u>white hairs</u> unto a quiet grave.
(Henry VI Part 3
Act II Scene 5)

King Henry:
Thy balm wash'd off wherewith thou wast
anointed:
No <u>bending knee</u> will call thee Caesar now.
(Henry VI Part 3
Act III Scene 1)

Timon:
This yellow slave (gold)
Will knit and break religions; bless th'
accurs'd;
Make the hoar leprosy ador'd; place thieves,
And give them title, <u>knee</u>, and approbation,
With senators on the bench...
(Timon of Athens
Act IV Scene 3)

Lear:
Conferring them on younger <u>strengths</u> –
(King Lear
Act I Scene 1)

Metellus:
O let us have him, for his <u>silver hairs</u>
Will purchase us a good opinion.
(Julius Caesar
Act II scene 1)

Neologism: **[ne O lo gism; Latin, *neo*, new and *logos*, word]**

New words. English language grew at an explosive rate during the Elizabethan age. Additions from

Greek and Latin were encouraged and sought out as a means of constantly enriching the language. At one time Shakespeare was credited with inventing many more words than now as new data bases have discovered other first usages, but according to Jonathan Bate ("The Mirror of Life" p40) Shakespeare is credited with coining among others, these words we still use today:

The verbs:

Torture
Misquote
Gossip
Swagger
Blanket
Champion
Puke

The nouns:

Critic
Mountaineer
Pageantry
Eyeball

The adjectives:

Fashionable
Unreal
Bloodstained
Deafening
Majestic
Domineering

The adverbs:

Instinctively
Obsequiously

Noema: **[no E ma; Greek, *noema,* a thought]**

(Puttenham's term: 'the figure of Close Conceit')

Overly subtle or obscure speech. **Enigma** is a related figure. **Noema** is a particularly imaginative way to present madness or mental confusion and consequently is found in the speech of characters like Ophelia, Hamlet, Edgar and Lear as they fall into an insanity (real or feigned) that reveals deep symbolic meaning.

King:
How do you, pretty lady?

Ophelia:
Well, God dild you! They say the owl was a baker's daughter. Lord, we know what we are, but know not what we may be. . . .God be at your table!

(Hamlet
Act IV Scene 5)

Rosencrantz:
Take you me for a sponge, my lord?

Hamlet:
Ay, sir, that soaks up the king's countenance, his rewards, his authorities. But such officers do the king best service in the end, he keeps them like an apple in the corner of his jaw, first mouthed to be last swallowed – when he needs what you have gleaned, it is but squeezing you, and, sponge, you shall be dry again.

Rosencrintz:
I understand you not, my lord.

(Hamlet.

Act IV Scene 2)

Lear:
Thou were better in a grave than to answer with thy uncovered body to the skies. Is man no more than this? Consider him well. Thou ow'st the worm no silk, the beast no hide, the sheep no wool, the cat no perfume, Ha! Here's three on's are sophisticated: thou are the thing itself. Unaccomodated man is no more but such a poor, bare, forked animal as thou art. Off, off you lendings! Come,unbutton here.

Fool:
Prithee, nuncle, be contented; 'tis a naughty night to swim in!

[Sees Gloucester approaching with a torch]

Now a little fire in a wild field were like an old lecher's heart—a small spark, all the rest on's body cold. Look, here comes a walking fire.

Edgar;
This is the foul Flibbertigibbet. He begins at curfew, and walks till first cock. He gives the web and the pin, squinies the eye, and makes the harelip; mildews the white wheat, and hurts the poor creature of the earth.
S'Withold footed thrice the 'old:
He met the Nightmare and her nine fold;
Bid her alight
And her troth plight—
And aroint thee, witch, aroint thee!
(King Lear

Act III Scene 4)

Onomatopoeia: [ON o ma to PEE a; Greek, *onoma*, a name, *poiein*, to make]

(Puttenham's term: 'the New Namer')

Words which sound like the entities they name.

Lear:
Blow, winds, and crack your cheeks! Rage!
Blow!
You cataracts and hurricanes, spout. . .
And thou, all-shaking thunder,
Strike flat the thick rotundity o'th' world,
Crack Nature's moulds.
(King Lear
Act III Scene 2)

For more examples, see **Onomatopoeia** in **Part I**

Orcos: [OR kus; Greek, *orcos*, oath]

An oath which confirms what one has affirmed or denied. The entire first one hundred and sixty lines of *Love's Labour's Lost* is an argument over an oath, one which Berowne considers to foolish to sign or swear to. Shakespeare uses the swearing of an oath **(orcos)** to increase to the highest degree the importance of the act being sworn to; it is therefore a crucial emotional and dramatic device. Note in each of the examples below, the use of **irmus**; that is the wording of the oath (**orcos**) is delayed until the end of the speech, thus heightening its importance.

Hermia:
My good Lysander,
I swear to thee by Cupid's strongest bow,

By his best arrow with the golden head,
By the simplicity of Venus' doves,
By that which knitteth souls and prospers loves,
And by that fire which burned the Carthage queen
When the false Troyan under sail was seen,
By all the vows that ever men have broke—
In number more than ever women spoke—
In that same place thou hast appointed me,
Tomorrow truly will I meet with thee.
(A Midsummer Night's Dream Act I Scene 1)

Hamlet:
Come hither, gentlemen,
And lay your hands again upon my sword.
Swear by my sword,
Never to speak of this that you have heard.

Ghost:
[beneath] Swear by his sword!

Hamlet:
Well said, old mole! Canst work i'th'earth so fast?
A worthy pioneer! Once more remove, good friends.

Horatio:
O day and night, but this is wondrous strange!

Hamlet:
And therefore as a stranger give it welcome.
There are more things in heaven and earth, Horatio,
Than are dreamt of in your philosophy.

But come—
Here, as before, never, so help you mercy
(How strange or odd some'er I bear myself,
As I perchance hereafter shall think meet
To put an antic disposition on)
That you at such times seeing me, never shall
With arms encumbered thus, or this head-shake,
Or by pronouncing of some doubtful phrase,
As 'Well, well, we know,'; or 'We could an if we would,'
Or 'If we list to speak,' or 'There be an if they might,'
Or such ambiguous giving out, to note
That you know aught of me—this do swear,
So grace and mercy at your most need help you!

Ghost: [beneath]
Swear.

Hamlet:
Rests, rest, perturbed spirit! [they swear]
(Hamlet Act I Scene 5)

Iago:
Patience, I say; your mind perhaps may change.

Othello:
Never, Iago: like to the Pontic sea,
Whose current and compulsive course
Ne'er feels retiring ebb, but keeps due on
To the Propontic and the Hellespont;
Even so my bloody thoughts, with a violent pace

Shall ne'er look back, ne'er ebb to humble
love,
Till that a capable and wide revenge
Swallow them up. Now, by yond marble
heaven,
In the due reverence of a sacred vow
[Kneels]
I here engage my words.

Iago:
Do not rise yet.
[Kneels]
Witness you ever-burning lights above,
You elements that clip us round about,
Witness that here Iago doth give up
The execution of his wit, hands, heart,
To wronged Othello's service! Let him
command,
And to obey shall be without remorse,
What bloody business ever.
(Othello
Act III Scene 3)

Panegyric: **[pa na GY rik; Greek, *panegyrikos*, fit for a public assembly or festival]**

A formal, laudatory speech extolling someone's achievements. A eulogy is often a **panegyric** for the dead. The speeches of Brutus and Mark Antony over the body of Caesar have elements of **panegyric.** Kate Hotspur's (Lady Percy's) memory of her husband results in a spontaneous **panegyric**, as does Cleopatra's description of her dream of Antony. To express a **panagyric** the speaker often uses **simile**, **metaphor**, **synonymia, hyperbole**, and other colorful figures. See a similar figure,

Encomium, for more examples.

Lady Percy:
O, yet, for God's sake, go not to these wars!
The time was, father, that you broke your word,
When you were more endeared to it than now,
When your own Percy, when my heart's dear Harry,
Threw many a northward look to see his father
Bring up his powers—but he did long in vain.
Who then persuaded you to stay at home?
There were two honors lost, yours and your son's.
For yours, the God of heaven brighten it!
For his, it stuck upon him, as the sun
In the grey vault of heaven, and by his light
Did all the chivalry of England move
To do brave acts. He was indeed the glass
Wherein the noble youth did dress themselves.
He had no legs that practiced not his gait;
And speaking thick, which nature made his blemish,
Became the accents of the valiant,
For those that could speak low and tardily
Would turn their own perfection to abuse,
To seem like him: so that in speech, in gait,
In diet, in affections of delight,
In military rules, humours of blood,
He was the mark and glass, copy and book,
That fashioned others. And him, O wondrous him!
O miracle of men! Him did you leave,
Second to none, unseconded by you,
To look upon the hideous god of war
In disadvantage, to abide a field

Where nothing but the sound of Hotspur's
name
Did seem defensible: so you left him.
Never, O never, do his ghost the wrong
To hold your honour more precise and nice
With others than with him! Let them alone:
The marshal and the archbishop are strong:
Had my sweet Harry had but half their
numbers,
To-day might I, hanging on Hotspur's neck
Have talked of Monmouth's grave.
(Henry IV Part II
Act II Scene 2)

It is interesting to observe the similarity of imagery between Kate Percy's speech above, and Ophelia's below. *Henry IV Part II* was written about 1598 and *Hamlet* about 1600.

Ophelia:
O, what a noble mind is here o'erthrown!
The courtier's, soldier's, scholar's, eye,
tongue, sword,
Th'expectancy and rose of the fair state,
The glass of fashion and the mould of form,
Th'observed of all observers, quite quite
down,
And I of ladies most deject and wretched,
That sucked the honey of his music vows,
Now see that noble and most sovereign reason
Like sweet bells jangled, out of tune and
harsh,
That unmatched form and feature of blown
youth,
Blasted with ecstasy! O, woe is me!
T'have seen what I have seen, see what I see!
(Hamlet

Act III Scene 1)

Cleopatra:
I dreamed there was an Emperor Antony.
O, such another sleep, that I might see
But such another man!. . .
His face was as the heavens, and therein stuck
A sun and moon, which kept their course and
lighted
The little O, the earth. . . .
His legs bestrid the ocean, his reared arm
Crested the world: his voice was propertied
As all the tuned spheres, and that to friends;
But when he meant to quail and shake the orb,
He was a rattling thunder. For his bounty,
There was no winter in't; an autumn 'twas
That grew the more by reaping: his delights
Were dolphin-like, they showed his back
above
The element they lived in: in his livery
Walked crown and crownets; realms and
islands were
As plates dropped from his pocket.

Dolabella:
Cleopatra!

Cleopatra:
Think you there was, or might be, such a man
As this I dreamed of?

Dolabella:
Gentle madam, no.

Cleopatra:
You lie, up to the hearing of the gods.
But if there be, or ever were, one such,

It's past the size of dreaming: nature wants
stuff
To vie such forms with Fancy, yet t'imagine

Condemning shadows quite.
(Antony and Cleopatra
Act V Scene 2)

Paradiastole: [PA ra di AS to le; Greek, *paradiastole,* a putting together of dissimilar things; *para*, side-by-side, *diastole*, separation, distinction]

(Puttenham's term: 'the Curry Fauell')

The use of flattery to calm or soothe, often by euphemistically replacing a negative word with something more pleasant, i. e. calling a 'great riot' a 'youthful prank'. Sometimes **paradiastole** involves distinguishing two meanings of the same word, as claiming 'I was in charge of the oversight in this case', if 'oversight' means 'supervision' but not if 'oversight' means 'mistake'. The opposite of **paradiastole** is **meiosis** where one denigrates or diminishes some one or something. The encounters between Prince Hal and Falstaff are filled with both figures in the example below.

Falstaff: [pretending to be Hal's father Henry IV]
. . . *there is a virtuous man* **[paradiastole]**
whom I have often noted in thy company, but
I know not his name.

Prince:
What manner of man, an it like your majesty?

Falstaff:
A goodly portly man, I'faith, and a corpulent, of a cheerful look, a pleasing eye, and a most noble carriage, and as I think his age some fifty, or by'r lady inclining to threescore. And now I remember me, his name is Falstaff. If that man should be lewdly given, he deceiveth me; for, Harry, I see virtue in his looks . . .
[**paradiastole**]

Prince:
Dost thou speak like a king? Do thou stand for me, and I'll play my father.
[speaking as the King]
Now, Harry whence come you?

Falstaff: [as the Prince]
My noble lord, from Eastcheap.

Prince:
The complaints I hear of thee are grievous.
[**meiosis**]

Falstaff:
'Sblood, my lord, they are false: nay, I'll tickle ye for a young prince, I'faith.

Prince:
Swearest thou, ungracious boy? Henceforth ne'er look on me. Thou art violently carried away from grace, there is a devil haunts thee in the likeness of an old fat man, a tun of man is thy companion: why dost thou converse with that trunk of humours, that bolting-hutch of beastliness, that swollen parcel of dropsies, that huge bombard of sack, that stuffed cloak-bag of guts, that roasted Manningtree

ox with the pudding in his belly, that reverend vice, that grey iniquity, that father ruffian, that vanity in Years. Wherein is he good, but to taste sack and drink it? wherein neat and cleanly, but to carve a capon and eat it? wherein cunning, but in craft? Wherein crafty, but in villainy? Wherein villainous, but in all things? Wherein worthy, but in nothing?
[meiosis]

Falstaff:
I would your grace would take me with you. Whom means your grace?

Prince:
That villainous abominable misleader of youth, Falstaff, that old white-bearded Satan.
(Henry IV Part I
Act II Scene 4)

In the above example, a good deal of **hyperbole** is added to the **meiosis** and **paradiastole,** the result of each man trying to top the other in vivid description. In *Troilus and Cressida* we see the figure referred to internally when Ajax accuses Achilles of using **paradiastole** in the following example:

Ajax:
Yes, lion-sick, sick of proud heart. You may call it melancholy, if you will favor the man; but by my head, 'tis pride.
(Troilus and Cressida
Act II Scene 3)

Paradigma: [PA ra DIG ma; Greek, *para*, beside, beyond, and

***digma,* example]**

The use of example, particularly an example from the past to illuminate the present. "The Tudor rhetoricians called the general figure of similitude homoeosis and distinguished as its species icon, parabola, **paradigma,** and fable." (SUAL p143) Of the four, examples of **paradigma** are most easily found in Shakespeare's work. His examples are primarily from the classica, indicating how thoroughly classical literature permeated his education.

> *Fluellen:*
> *If you mark Alexander's life well, Harry of Monmouth's life is come after it indifferent well; for there is figures in all things. . . . As Alexander kill'd his friend Cleitus, being in his ales and cups, so also Harry Monmouth, being in his right wits and good judgments, turn'd away the fat knight.*
> *(Henry V*
> *Act IV Scene 7)*

> *Hamlet:*
> *To what base uses we may return, Horatio! Why may not imagination trace the noble dust of Alexander, till a'find it stopping a bung-hole. . . . as thus—Alexander died, Alexander was buried, Alexander returneth to dust, the dust is earth, of earth we make loam, and why of that loam whereto he was converted might they not stop a beer-barrel?*
> *Imperious Caesar, dead and turned to clay,*
> *Might stop a hole to keep the wind away.*
> *O, that the earth, which kept the world in awe,*

Should patch a wall t'expel the winter's flaw!
(Hamlet
Act V Scene 1)

Portia:
I grant I am a woman, but withal
A woman Lord Brutus took to wife:
I grant I am a woman, but withal
A woman well reputed, Cato's daughter.
Think you I am no stronger than my sex,
Being so fathered and so husbanded?
(Julius Caesar
Act II Scene 1)

Pistol:
These be good humours, indeed!
Shall pack horses
And hollow pampered jades of Asia,
Which cannot go but thirty mile a day,
Compare with Caesars and with Cannibals
And Trojan Greeks? Nay, rather damn them with
King Cerberus, and let the welkin roar.
Shall we fall foul for toys?
(Henry IV Part II
Act II Scene 4)

Paradoxon: **[pa ra DOX on; Greek, *para,* beyond, and *doxon*, opinion]**

(Puttenham's term: 'the Wondrer) "I wonder much to see . . ."

Often used to explore self-contradictory feelings, or to arouse wonder in the listener. As Puttenham notes, this figure often begins with the words 'I wonder'. In positing a dual reality **paradoxon** is akin to **irony** and **antithesis**, two of Shakespeare's favorite figures.

Benedick:
<u>I do much wonder</u> that one man seeing how much another man is a fool when he dedicates his behaviors to love, will, after he hath laughed at such shallow follies in others, become the argument of his own scorn by falling in love. And such a man is Claudio. I have known when there was no music with but the drum and the fife, and now had he rather hear the tabor and the pipe: I have known him when he would have walked ten mile afoot, to see a good armour, and now will he lie ten nights awake carving the fashion of a new doublet: he was wont to speak plain, and to the purpose (like an honest man and a soldier) and now is he turned orthography—his words are a very fantastical banquet, just so many strange dishes. <u>May I be so converted and see with these eyes? I can not tell—I think not</u>: I will not be sworn but love may transform me to an oyster, but I'll take my oath on it, till he have made an oyster of me, he shall never make me such a fool.
(Much Ado About Nothing Act II Scene 3)

Berowne:
No <u>face is fair</u> that is <u>not full so black</u>.

King:
O <u>paradox</u>! Black is the badge of hell,
The hue of dungeons, and the school of night

. . .

Berowne:

And therefore is she born to make black fair.
(Love's Labour's Lost
Act IV Scene 3)

Ophelia:
Could beauty, my lord, have better commerce than with honesty?

Hamlet:
Ay, truly, for the power of beauty will sooner transform honesty from what it is to a bawd than the force of honesty can translate beauty into its likeness. This was sometime a paradox, but now the time gives it proof.
(Hamlet
Act III Scene 1)

Witches:
Fair is foul, and foul is fair.
(Macbeth
Act I Scene 1)

Paragoge: **[pa ra GO ge; Greek, a drawing out, from *para*, beyond, and *agein*, to lead]**

Adding a syllable to the ends of words which often gives an informal, casual style to the discourse or dialogue, or aids in the desired rhythm as 'Sweetie' or 'Dearie'.

Ophelia:
You must sing, 'Adown adown,' an you call him adown –a.
(Hamlet
Act IV Scene 7)

Hostess:

I'faith, sweetheart, methinks now you are in an excellent good temporality; your pulsidge beats as extraordinarily as heart would desire, and your colour, I warrant you, is as red as any rose, in good truth, la!
(Henry IV Part II
Act II Scene 4)

Paralepsis: **[pa ra LEP sis; Greek, *paralepsis*, to leave on one side, pass by, disregard, omission]**

Going on and on about something after promising to say nothing about it. In this figure a character reveals his subject while claiming to pass it over. Shakespeare often uses this technique to establish comedic characterizations.

Polonius:
Madame, I swear I use no art at all.
That he is mad, 'tis true; 'tis true, 'tis pity;
And pity 'tis 'tis true; a foolish figure
But farewell it, for I will use no art.
Mad let us grant him, then; and now remains
That we find out the cause of this effect,
Or rather say, the cause of this defect,
For this effect defective comes by cause;
Thus it remains and the remainder thus.
(Hamlet
Act II Scene 2)

Grumio:
Tell thou the tale: but hadst thou not crossed me, thou shouldst have heard how her horse fell, and she under her horse; thou shouldst have heard in how miry a place, how she was bemoiled, how he left her with the horse upon

her, how he beat me because her horses stumbled, how she waded through the dirt to pluck him off me; how he swore, how she prayed that never prayed before; how I cried, how the horses ran away, how her bridle was burst; how I lost my crupper—with many things of worthy memory, which now shall die in oblivion, and thou return unexperienced to thy grave.

(The Taming of the Shrew
Act IV Scene 1)

Antony:
Let but the common hear this testament,
Which (pardon me) I do not mean to read,
And they would go and kiss dead Caesar's wounds . . .
Have patience, gentle friends; I must not read it.
It is not meet you know how Caesar lov'd you. . . .
'Tis good you know not that you are his heirs.

(Julius Caesar
Act III Scene 2)

Paranomasia: [pa ra no MA si a; Greek, *para*, beside, *nomasia*, naming; *paranomazein*, to alter in naming]

A punning figure where words are almost identical in sound though not meaning. See the other punning figures: **Antanaclasis**, **Syllepsis** and **Asteismus**.

Lysander:
For lying so, Hermia, I do not lie.

(A Midsummer Night's Dream
Act II Scene 2)

Antony:
All length is <u>torture</u>. Since the <u>torch</u> is out,
Lie down and stray no further.
(Antony and Cleopatra
Act IV Scene 14)

Lady Macbeth:
If he do bleed,
I'll <u>gild</u> the faces of the grooms withal,
For it must seem their <u>guilt</u>.
(Macbeth
Act II Scene 2)

Desdemona:
I cannot say '<u>whore</u>',
It doth ab<u>hor</u> me now I speak the word.
(Othello
Act IV Scene 2)

Parataxis: **[pa ra TAX is; Greek, placing side by side from *para*, beside, and *tassein* to place]**

Presenting words, phrases or clauses in an equal instead of subordinate position. A favorite example in Latin is Caesar's Veni, vivi, vici. This figure can display **asyndeton** (no use of conjunctions, as in Caesar's quote above, so familiar to every Elizabethan schoolboy) or **polysyndeton** – the use of more conjunctions than usual (...and...and...and). Otherwise defined as clauses or phrases arranged independently in coordinate, rather than a subordinate, construction).

Fairy:
<u>Over hill, over dale,</u>
<u>Thorough bush, thorough briar</u>
<u>Over park, over pale,</u>

> *Thorough flood, thorough fire,*
> *I do wander everywhere. . . .*
> *(A Midsummer Night's Dream Act II Scene 1)*

> *Queen:*
> *I took a costly jewel from my neck,*
> *A heart it was, bound in with diamonds,*
> *And threw it towards thy land: the sea received it,*
> *And so I wish'd thy body might my heart:*
> *And even with this I lost fair England's view*
> *And bid mine eyes be packing with my heart*
> *And call'd them blind and dusky spectacles,*
> *For losing ken of Albion's wished coast.*
> *(Henry VI Part 2 Act III Scene 2)*

Parimion: **(par I mi on; Puttenham's term: 'the figure of Like Letter)**
See **Alliteration** in **Part I.**

Parison: **[PAR i son; Greek, *parison,* exactly or evenly balanced; *para,* beside, *isos*, equal]**

(Puttenham's term: 'the figure of Even')

Equal structures in successive clauses or sentences; word matching against word. Puttenham advises writers not to use more than three or four of these equal short clauses for maximum effectiveness.

Lanham distinguishes i**socolon** from **parison** by limiting **parison** to "long phrases or clauses in parallel construction sometimes with similar sounds in similar places in the parallel phrases or clauses" (HRT, p62) and gives the following example:

Nathaniel:
Your reasons at dinner have been sharp and sententious; pleasant without scurrility, witty without affection, audacious without impudency, learned without opinion, and strange without heresy.
(Love's Labour's Lost
Act V Scene 1)

O, no, it is an ever-fixed mark
That looks on tempests and is never shaken;
It is the star to every wand'ring bark
Whose worth's unknown, although his height be taken.
(Sonnet #116)

If snow be white, why then her breasts are dun.
If hairs be wires, black wires grow on her head.
(Sonnet #130)

Partitio: **[par TI ti o; Latin, division into parts. See Merismus**

Periphrasis: **[pe RIF ra sis; Greek, *peri*, about and *phrazein*, to speak]**

(Puttenham's term: 'the figure of Ambiage')

A figure that "**will not in one or a few words expresse that thing which we desire to have known but do choose rather to do it by many words.**" Puttenham notes that this is a figure easily abused. Acknowledging this, Shakespeare uses it to establish pedantic, comedic characters. Compare with **Auxesis**, **Bomphiologia**, **Cacozelia** and **Hyperbole**.

> *Holofernes:*
> *This is a gift that I have, simple, simple; a foolish, extravagant spirit, full of forms, figures, shapes, objects, ideas, apprehensions, motions, revolutions. These are begot in the ventricle of memory, nourished in the womb of pia mater, and delivered upon the mellowing of occasion. But the gift is good in those in whom it is acute, and I am thankful for it.*
> *(Love's Labour's Lost Act IV Scene 2)*

> *Armado:*
> *I give thee thy liberty, set thee from durance, and in lieu thereof impose on thee nothing but this [he proffers him a letter] Bear this significant to the country maid Jaquenetta. . There is remuneration—for the best ward of mine honour is rewardingmy dependents.*
> *(Love's Labour's Lost Act III Scene 1)*

> *Falstaff:*
> *I have writ me here a letter to her: and here another to Page's wife; who even now gave me good eyes too; examined my parts with most judicious oeillades: sometimes the beam of her view gilded my foot. . . sometimes my portly belly. . .O she did so course o'er my exteriors with such a greedy intention, that the appetite of her eye did seem to scorch me up like a burning glass. ..Here's another letter to her; she bears the purse, too: she's a*

region in Guiana: all gold and bounty. . . I will be cheaters to them both, and they shall be exchequers to me: they shall be my East and West Indies and I will trade to them both.
(The Merry Wives of Windsor
Act I Scene 3)

Pleonasmus (surplusage): [ple on AS mus; Greek, *pleonasmos*, from *pleon*, more, excess]

Needless repetition of what is has already been expressed; redundancy.

Pistol:
He hears with ears.

Evans:
. . . What phrase is this? 'He hears with ear'?
(The Merry Wives of Windsor
Act I Scene 1)

Clown:
His biting is immortal. Those that do die of it do seldom or never recover.
(Antony and Cleopatra
Act V Scene 2)

Nurse:
I saw the wound, I saw it with mine eyes.
(Romeo and Juliet
Act III Scene 2)

Ploce: [PLO ce; Greek, *ploke,* a plaiting or braiding, from *plekein,* to braid]

(Puttenham's term: 'the Doubler' Puttenham defines it as "the speedie iteration of one word

with some little intermission." (p.201))

The repetition of a repeated word, interrupted by a word or two, sometimes with a modification of meaning. See also **Diacope** .

Love is too young to know what conscience is
Yet who knows not conscience is born of love?
(Sonnet #151)

Egeus:
Enough, enough, my lord; you have enough!
I beg the law, the law upon his head!
They would have stol'n away, they would, Demitrius.
(A Midsummer Night's Dream Act IV Scene 1)

King Henry:
Ah, what a life were this! how sweet! how lovely!
Gives not the hawthorn-bush a sweeter shade
To shepherds looking on their silly sheep,
Than doth a rich embroider'd canopy
To kings that fear their subjects' treachery?
O, yes, it doth; a thousand-fold it doth.
(Henry VI Part 3 Act II, Scene 5)

Queen:
Be thou assured, if words be made of breath,
And breath of life, I have no life to breathe
What thou hast said to me.
(Hamlet Act III, Scene 4)

Polyptoton: [po lyp TO ton; Greek, *poly*, much or many, and *piptein*, to fall]

Repetition of a word where the second usage is not identical with the first but comes from the same root.

Helena:
I followed fast, but faster did he fly.
(Midsummer Night's Dream
Act III Scene 2)

Caesar:
I could be well moved, if I were as you;
If I could pray to move, prayers would move me,
But I am constant as the northern star.'
(Julius Caesar
Act III Scene 1)

Troilus:
The Greeks are strong and skilful in their strength,
Fierce to their skill, and to their fierceness valiant.
(Troilus and Cressida
Act I Scene 1)

And that unfair
Which fairly doth excel.
(Sonnet #5)

Polysyndeton: [po ly SYN de ton; Greek, *poly*, much or many, and *syndein*, to bind together]

(Puttenham's term: 'couple clause')

Using many conjunctions. See also **Parataxis** and **Parison** for structures which can be a result of **polysyndeton.**

Puck:
<u>And</u> neigh, <u>and</u> bark, <u>and</u> grunt, <u>and</u> roar, <u>and</u> burn,
Like horse, hound, hog, bear, fire, at every turn.
(A Midsummer Night's Dream Act III Scene 1)

Above Shakespeare uses **polysyndeton** in the first line and **asyndeton** in the second (leaving out the conjunction 'and'). The effect is to rapidly increase Puck's rhythm at the very end of his speech.

Tired with all these, for restful death I cry,
As, to behold desert a beggar born,
<u>And</u> needy nothing trimm'd in jollity,
<u>And</u> purest faith unhappily forsworn,
<u>And</u> guilded honour shamefully misplaced,
<u>And</u> maiden virtue rudely strumpeted,
<u>And</u> right perfection wrongfully disgraced,
<u>And</u> strength by limping sway disabled,
<u>And</u> art made tongue-tied by authority,
<u>And</u> folly doctor-like controlling skill,
<u>And</u> simple truth miscall'd simplicity,
<u>And</u> captive good attending captain ill:
Tired with all these, from these would I be gone,
Save that, to die, I leave my love alone.
(Sonnet #66)

As the 'and' above begins each line this **poly-syndeton** is also an example of **Anaphora.**

1 Petitioner:
Mine is, an't please your grace, against John Goodman, my lord cardinal's man, for keeping my house, <u>and</u> lands, <u>and</u> wife <u>and</u> all, from me.
(Henry VI Part 2
Act 1 Scene 3)

Clifford:
Now, Richard, I am with thee here alone:
This is the hand that stabb'd thy father York;
<u>And</u> this the hand that slew thy brother Rutland;
<u>And</u> here's the heart that triumphs in their death
<u>And</u> cheers these hands that slew thy sire and brother
To execute the like upon thyself;
<u>And</u> so, have at thee!
(Henry VI Part 3
Act II Scene 4)

Bottom:
<u>That</u> liv'd, <u>that</u> lov'd, <u>that</u> lik'd, <u>that</u> look'd, with cheer.
(A Midsummer Night's Dream
Act V)

Pragmatographia: [prag ma to GRA fi a; Greek, *pragma*, business and *graphia*, writing]

The vivid description of an event or action; important dramatically when a character must report something crucial that has happened off-stage. Each speech below in its entirety is an example of **pragmatographia.**

Gremio:
I'll tell you, Sir Lucentio: when the priest
Should ask if Katharine should be his wife,
'Ay, by gogs-wouns,' quoth he, and swore so loud,
That all-amazed the priest let fall the book,
And as he stooped again to take it up,
This mad-brained bridegroom took him such a cuff,
That down fell priest and book, and book and priest.
'Now take them up,' quoth he, 'if any list . . .
He calls for wine – 'A health,' quoth he, as if
He had been aboard, carousing to his mates
After a storm—quaffed off the muscadel,
And threw the sops all in the sexton's face;
Having no other reason
But that his beard grew thin and hungerly,
And seemed to ask him sops as he was drinking.
This done, he took the bride about the neck,
And kissed her lips with such a clamorous smack,
That at the parting all the church did echo:
And I seeing this came thence for very shame,
And after me I know the rout is coming.
Such a mad marriage never was before. . .
(The Taming of the Shrew
Act III Scene 2)

Oliver:
When last the young Orlando parted from you
He left a promise to return again
Within an hour, and pacing through the forest,
Chewing the food of sweet and bitter fancy,

Lo, what befel! he threw his eye aside,
And mark what object did present itself!
Under an oak, whose boughs were mossed
with age
And high top bald with dry antiquity,
A wretched ragged man, o'ergrown with hair,
Lay sleeping on his back: about his neck
A green and gilded snake had wreathed itself,
Who with her head nimble in threats
approached
The opening of his mouth; but suddenly
Seeing Orlando, it unlinked itself,
And with indented glides did slip away
Into a bush: under which bush's shade
A lioness, with udders all drawn dry,
Lay couching, head on ground, with catlike
watch
When that the sleeping man should stir; for
'tis
The royal disposition of that beast
To prey on nothing that doth seem as dead:
This seen, Orlando did approach the man,
And found it was his brother, his elder
brother.

(As You Like It
Act IV Scene 3)

Casca:
Are not you moved, when all the sway of earth
Shapes like a thing unfirm? O Cicero,
I have seen tempests, when the scolding winds
Have rived the knotty oaks, and I have seen
Th'ambitious ocean swell and rage and foam,
To be exalted with the threat'ning clouds;
But never till to-night, never till now,
Did I go through a tempest dropping fire. . . .
A common slave—you know him well by

sight—
Held up his left hand, which did flame and burn
Like twenty torches joined, and yet his hand
Not sensible of fire remained unscorched.
Besides—I ha' not since put up my sword—
Against the Capitol I met a lion,
Who glazed upon me and went surly by
Without annoying me: and there were drawn
Upon a heap a hundred ghastly women
Transformed with their fear, who swore they saw
Men all in fire walk up and down the streets.
And yesterday the bird of night did sit
Even at noon-day upon the market-place,
Hooting and shrieking.
(Julius Caesar
Act I Scene 3)

Prolepsis: **[pro LEP sis; Greek, *prolepsis*, an anticipating; *pro,* before and *lambanein*, to take]**

(Puttenham's term: 'the Propounder or Explainer')

A general statement followed by many particulars. Alternatively, a figure where the writer first suggests a defect or lack which is then supplied or remedied or explained. Much of Petruchio's relationship with Katharina is expressed through prolepsis:

Petruchio:
I will attend her here,
And woo her with some spirit when she comes.
Say that she rail, why then I'll tell her plain
She sings as sweetly as a nightingale:

Say that she frown, I'll say she looks as clear
As morning roses newly washed with dew:
Say she be mute and will not speak a word,
Then I'll commend her volubility
And say she uttereth piercing eloquence:
If she do bid me pack, I'll give her thanks,
As though she bid me stay by her a week:
If she deny to wed, I'll crave the day
When I shall ask the banns, and when be married.

(The Taming of the Shrew Act II Scene 1)

According to Sister Miriam Joseph **prolepsis** consists of a general statement "amplified by dividing it into parts. . . ." (SUAL,p116)

Hermia:
If then true lovers have been ever crossed,
It stands as an edict in destiny:
Then let us teach our trial patience,
Because it is a customary cross,
As due to love, as thoughts, and dreams, and sighs,
Wishes and tears, poor Fancy's followers.

(A Midsummer Night's Dream Act I Scene 1)

Arviragus:
We are beastly: subtle as the fox for prey,
Like warlike as the wolf for what we eat.
Our valour is to chase what flies; our cage
We make a choir, as doth the prison'd bird,
And sing our bondage freely.

(Cymbeline Act III Scene 3)

Lear:
No, no, no, no! Come, let's away to prison:
We two alone will sing like birds I'th'cage;
When thou dost ask me blessing, I'll kneel down
And ask of thee forgiveness. So we'll live
And pray and sing, and tell old tales, and laugh
At gilded butterflies, and hear poor rogues
Talk of court news; and we'll talk with them too—
Who loses and who wins, and who's in, and who's out—
And take upon's the mystery of things,
As if we were God's spies; and we'll wear out,
In a walled prison, packs and sects of great ones
That ebb and flow by th'moon.
(King Lear
Act V Scene 3)

Richard:
I have been studying how I may compare
This prison where I live unto the world:
And because the world is populous,
And here is not a creature but myself,
I cannot do it. Yet I'll hammer it out.
My brain I'll prove the female to my soul,
My soul the father, and these two beget
A generation of still-breeding thoughts:
And these same thoughts people this little world,
In humours like the people of this world:
For no thought is contented: the better sort,
As thoughts of things divine, are intermixed

With scruples, and do set the word itself
Against the word. . . .
(Richard II
Act V Scene 5)

Prosonomasia: [pro so no MA si a; Greek, *prosonomasia,* a naming; *pros,* to and *anomazein* to name

(Puttenham's term: 'the Nicknamer')

A by-name given in sport, not a surname given in earnest purpose.

Nuncle the Fool's name for King Lear.
Hotspur for Henry Percy
Puck for Robin Goodfellow

Prosopographia: [pro so no GRA fi a; Greek, *prosopon*, face, and *graphia*, writing]

The vivid description of a person.

Horatio:
Two nights together had these gentlemen,
Marcellus and Barnardo, on their watch
In the dead waste and middle of the night,
Been thus encountered. A figure like your father
Armed at point exactly, cap-a-pe,
Appears before them, and with solemn march,
Goes slow and stately by them; thrice he walked
By their oppressed and fear-surprised eyes
Within his truncheon's length, whilst they distilled
Almost to jelly with the act of fear,
Stand dumb and speak not to him. . . .

It lifted up its head, and did address
Itself to motion like as it would speak:
But even then the morning cock crew loud,
And at the sound it shrunk in haste away
And vanished from our sight.
(Hamlet
Act I Scene 2)

Ophelia:
My lord, as I was sewing in my closet,
Lord Hamlet with his doublet all unbraced,
No hat upon his head, his stockings fouled
Ungart'red, and down-gyved to his ankle,
Pale as a shirt, his knees knocking each other,
And with a look so piteous in purport
As if he had been loosed out of hell
To speak of horrors – he comes before me.
(Hamlet
Act II Scene 1)

Queen:
There is a willow grows askant the brook,
That shows its hoar leaves in the glassy stream,
Therewith fantastic garlands did she make
Of crow-flowers, nettles, daisies, and long purples
That liberal shepherds give a grosser name,
But our cold maids do dead men's fingers call them.
There on the pendent boughs her crownet weeds
Clamb'ring to hang, an envious sliver broke,
When down her weedy trophies and herself
Fell in the weeping brook. Her clothes spread wide,
And mermaid-like awhile they bore her up,

Which time she chanted snatches of old lauds,
As one incapable of her own distress,
Or like a creature native and indued
Unto that element. But long it could not be
Till that her garments, heavy with their drink,
Pulled the poor wretch from her melodious
lay
To muddy death.
(Hamlet
Act IV Scene 7)

Prosopopoei: [pro so PO pi a; Greek, from *prosopon.* face, person and *poiein*, to make]

The attribution of human qualities to inanimate or non-human creatures, different from **personification** (**Part I**) in that with **prosopopoei** the inanimate object remains as it is, does not become a person, even though the ability to feel or to have other human qualities is attributed to it.

Arthur:
There is no malice in this burning coal;
The breath of heaven hath blown his spirit out
And strew'd repentant ashes on his head.

Hubert:
But with my breath I can revive it, boy.

Arthur:
And if you do, you will but make it blush
And glow with shame of your proceedings,
Hubert . . . .
All things that you should use to do me wrong
Deny their office. Only you do lack
That mercy which fierce fire and iron extends,
Creatures of note for mercy-lacking uses.
(King John

Act IV Scene 1)

Gertrude:
When down her weedy trophies and herself
Fell into the weeping brook.
(Hamlet
Act IV Scene 7)

But as the earth doth weep, the sun being set,
Each flower moist'ned like a melting eye. . .

.

(The Rape of Lucrece
Verse 176)

Sarcasmus: (sar KAS mus; Greek, *sarcasmos*, a bitter laugh, from *sarkazein*, to tear flesh like a dog)

(Puttenham's term: 'the Bitter Taunt')

Open, bitter, jibe; the mockery of a person, idea, or action.

Kent: [to Oswald who pretends not to recognize him]
What a brazen-faced varlet art thou, to deny thou knowest me! Is it two days since I tripped up thy heels and beat thee before the king? Draw, you rogue; for, though it be night, yet the moon shines. I'll make a sop o'th' moonshine of you, you whore-son cullionly barber-monger. Draw!
(King Lear
Act II Scene 2)

King Richard:
Ha? Am I king? 'tis so—but Edward lives.

Buckingham:
True, noble prince.

King Richard:
O bitter consequence!
That Edward should live 'true noble prince'!
<u>Cousin, thou was not wont to be so dull</u>.
Shall I be plain? I wish the bastards dead.
And I would have it suddenly performed.
What say'st thou now? Speak suddenly, be brief.

Buckinghim:
Your grace may do your pleasure.

Richard:
<u>Tut, tut, thou art all ice, thy kindness freezes</u>.
(Richard III
Act IV Scene 1)

Thersites: [to Ajax who has threatened to beat him]
Do, do, <u>thou stool for a witch</u>! Ay, do, do, <u>thou sodden-witted</u> Lord! <u>Thou hast no more brain in thy head than I have in</u> <u>mine elbows</u>; <u>an assinego may tutor thee</u>. <u>Thou scurvy-valliant</u> ass! Thou art here but to thrash Trojans; as <u>thou art bought</u> <u>and sold among those of any wit, like a barbarian slave</u>.
If thou use to beat me, I will begin at thy heel and tell what thou art by inches, <u>thou thing of no bowels, thou</u>!
(Troilus and Cressida
Act II Scene 1)

Sillepsis: **see <u>syllepsis</u>**

Sinathroesmus: see Synathroesmus

Sinonimia: [si no NI mi a; Greek, of like meaning or like name]

(Puttenham's term: the figure of Store)

A figure of repetition where different words or clauses are used which mean the same thing. See **Synonym** in **Part I.**

King [reading a letter from Armado]
Then for the place Where? where I
mean I did encounter that obscene and most
prepostrous event, that draweth from
my snow-white pen the ebon-colored Ink,
which here thou <u>viewest</u>, <u>beholdest</u>, <u>surveyest</u>,
or <u>seest</u>.
(Love's Labour's Lost
Act I Scene 1)

Macbeth:
But now I am <u>cabin'd</u>, <u>cribb'd</u>, <u>confin'd</u>,
<u>bound in</u>
To saucy doubts and fears.
(Macbeth
Act III Scene 4)

Solicismus: [so le SIS mos; Greek, *soloikos*, speaking incorrectly]

The ignorant misuse of grammar, cases, genders and tenses. Shakespeare uses this device to establish comedic characters, especially those who try to prove their education by pretentious speech. Below, Dogberry is overjoyed that Leonato has asked him to examine his suspects himself, and he expresses this delight by attempting to sound particularly official.

> *Dogberry:*
> *Go good partner, go get you to Francis Seacoal, bid him bring his pen and inkhorn to the gaol: we are now* <u>*to examination*</u> *these men.*
>
> *(Much Ado About Nothing*
> *Act III Scene 4)*

In *Henry V* Nym and Pistol throw in words helter-skelter because they sound like what they would express. Sometimes one can make a direct connection with the word they really want, and sometimes not.

> *Nym:*
> *Faith, I will live so long as I may, that's the certain of it: and when I cannot live any longer, I will do as I may, that is my rest,* <u>*that is the rendez-vous of it*</u>*. . . .*
>
> *Hostess:*
> *As ever you come of women, come in quickly to Sir John. Ah, poor heart! he is so shaked of a burning quotidian tertian, that it is most lamentable to behold. Sweet men, come to him.*
>
> *Nym:*
> *The king hath run bad humours on the knight, that's the* <u>*even of it*</u>*.*
>
> *Pistol:*
> *Nym, thou hast spoke the right,*
> <u>*His heart is fracted and corroborate*</u>*.*
>
> *[for 'fractured' and 'coroborate'*

meaning strengthened – it must just have sounded good to Pistol!]

Nym:
The king is a good king, but it must be as it may: he passes some humours and careers.

Pistol:
Let us condole [for 'console'] the knight, for, lambkins, we will live.
(Henry V
Act II Scene 1)

The Clowns' solecisms revolve around the misuse or mispronunciations of words in the Gravediggers' scene.

1 Clown:
Is she to be buried in Christian burial when she willfully seeks her own salvation?

[for 'damnation' through committing suicide]

2 Clown:
I tell thee she is, therefore make her grave straight. The crowner hath sat on her,

[for 'the coroner has heard her case']
and finds it Christian burial.

1 Clown:
How can that be, unless she drowned herself in her own defense?

2 Clown:
Why, 'tis found so.

1 Clown:
It must be '<u>se offendendo,</u>' [for 'se defendendo'] it cannot be else.
For here lies the point, if I drown myself wittingly, it argues an act,
and an act hath three branches, it is to act, to do, and to perform— <u>argal,</u> [for 'ergo'] she drowned herself wittingly.
(Hamlet
Act V Scene 1)

Soriasmus: **[sor i AS mus; Greek, *soraismos*, heaping up]**

(Puttenham's term: the Mingle-Mangle)

A linguistic vice consisting of the misuse of foreign words ignorantly and affectedly inserted into one's speech. Shakespeare uses this to satirize pedants and those wanting to show off erudition.
Related to **Solicismus** above.
See **Bomphiologia** for more examples.

Stichomythia: **[sti ko MI thi a; Greek, *stichos*, a line, and *mythos,* speech or talk]**

Rapidly alternating single lines of dialogue, usually in contrast to speeches of some length. Shakespeare uses this device to pick up the rhythm and pace of a scene. **Stichomythic** lines always tell the director and the performers to create a sense of competition and one-ups-man-ship between the characters which is revealed technically by rapid pick-up of cues.
See **Stichomythia** in **Part I** for more examples. The scenes should be exhilarating for the actors to play and for the audience to hear.

Petruchio:
A herald, Kate? Oh put me in thy books.

Katharina:
What is your crest? A coxcomb?

Petruchio:
A combless cock, so Kate will be my hen

Katharina:
No cock of mine; you crow too like a craven.

Petruchio:
Nay, come, Kate, come, you must not look so sour.

Katharina :
It is my fashion when I see a crab.
(The Taming of the Shrew
Act II Scene 1)

Lady Anne:
I would I knew thy heart.

Gloucester:
'Tis figured in my tongue.

Lady Anne:
I fear me both are false.

Gloucester:
Then never man was true.

Lady Anne:
Well, well, put up your sword.

Gloucester:
Say, then, my peace is made.

Lady Anne:
That shall you know hereafter.

Gloucester:
But shall I live in hope?

Lady Anne:
All men, I hope, live so.

Gloucester:
Vouchsafe to wear this ring.

Lady Anne:
To take is not to give.
(Richard III
Act I Scene 2)

Hamlet:
Now, mother, what's the matter?

Gertrude:
Hamlet, thou hast thy father much offended.

Hamlet:
Mother, you have my father much offended

Gertrude:.
Come, come, you answer with an idle tongue.

Hamlet:
Go, go, you question with a wicked tongue.
(Hamlet
Act III Scene 4)

Surplusage **see Pleonasmus [Latin, *super,* above, and *plus,* more]**

Syllepsis: **[sil LEP sis; Greek, putting together, from *syllambanein*, to take together]**

(Puttenham's term: 'the Double Supply.')

"Like the man that serves many masters at once, being of strange Countries or kindreds."

From the Greek "taking together." Sometimes defined as one verb lacking congruence with at least one subject it governs, as "The Nobles and the King was taken." It differs from **zeugma** in that there is no mistaken congruence with **zeugma.** But Sister Miriam Joseph also identifies **syllepsis** as one of the four classic punning figures. **Syllepsis** uses a word having simultaneously two separate meanings. The other punning figures are **Antanaclasis**, **Asteismus,** and **Paranomasia.** Shakespearean examples are somewhat rare for **syllepsis** in the first usage (where the verb lacks congruence with one of the subjects), but examples are plentiful for the punning definition. The first two examples below show multiple subjects with the verb lacking congruence; the other examples illustrate the punning definiton.

Princess:
This field shall hold me, and so hold your vow:
<u>*Nor God nor I delights*</u> *in perjur'd men.*
(Love's Labour's Lost

Act V Scene 2)

King:

What should be said?
If thou canst like this creature as a maid,
I can create the rest: virtue and she
Is her own dower; honour and wealth, from me.

(Measure for Measure
Act II Scene 3)

Duchess:
Love loving not itself, none other can.

(Richard II
Act V Scene 3)

Doctor: [observing Lady Macbeth sleep walking]
Well, well, well.

Gentlewoman:
Pray God it be, sir.

(Macbeth
Act V Scene 1)

Falstaff:
At a word, hang no more about me. I am no gibbet for you.

(Merry Wives of Windsor
Act II Scene 2)

Beatrice:
If the Prince be too important, tell him there is measure in everything, and so dance out the answer.

(Much Ado About Nothing

Act II Scene 1)

Symploce: **[SYM plo ce; Greek, from *syn*, together, and *piekein*, to twine]**

(Puttenham's term: 'the figure of Replie') See also **Epinome.**

According to **Puttenham**, when one and the same word or phrase begins or ends many verses, but defined by Sister Miriam Joseph as a combination of **anaphora** (beginning phrases with the same word) and **epistrophe** (ending phrases with the same word). According to Puttenham **symploce** is found in songs as follows:

Puttenham examples*:*

Desdemona:
Sing all a green willow
Willow, willow, willow
Ay me the green willow shall be my garland.
(Repeats at end of each verse)
(Othello
Act IV Scene 3)

Feste:
With a heigh ho, the wind and the rain. . .
And the rain it raineth every day.
(Repeats at the end of each verse)
(Twelfth Night
Act V Scene 1)

First and Second Page:
In spring time, in spring time
The only pretty ring time
When birds do sing

Hey ding a ding a ding
Hey ding a ding a ding
Sweet lovers love the spring.
(Repeats at the end of each verse)
(As You Like It
Act V Scene 2)

Sister Miriam Joseph's definition is illustrated by the example:

Brutus:
Who is here so base that would be a bondman? If any, speak; for him have I offended. Who is here so rude that would not be a Roman? If any, speak; for him have I offended. Who is here so vile that will not love his country? If any, speak; for him have I offended.
(Julius Caesar
Act III Scene 2)

Synathroesmus: [sin a THROE smus; Greek, from *syn*, together, with; collection, union]

An accumulation of individual items, making a long list of examples often leading to recapitulation and explanation. The opposite of **synathroesmus** is **prolepsis,** where the general statement comes first, followed by a string of examples.

Lysander:
Making it momentary, as a sound:
Swift as a shadow, short as any dream
Brief as the lightning in the collied night,
That (in a spleen) unfolds both heaven and earth,
And ere a man hath power to say, behold,

<u>The jaws of darkness do devour it up</u>:
<u>So quick bright things come to confusion</u>.
(A Midsummer Night's Dream
Act I Scene 1)

Lust is <u>perjured, murd'rous, bloody, full of</u>
<u>blame</u>
<u>Savage, extreme, rude, cruel, not to trust</u>.
(Sonnet # 129)

Ullyses:
The heavens themselves, the planets and this
centre,
Observe <u>degree, priority and place,</u>
<u>Insisture, course, proportion, season, form,</u>
<u>Office and custom</u>, in all like of order. . .
But when the planets
In evil mixture to disorder wander,
What <u>raging of the sea, shaking of earth,</u>
<u>Commotion in the winds, frights, changes,</u>
<u>horrors,</u>
<u>Divert and crack</u>, <u>rend and deracinate</u>
The unity and married calm of states
Quite from their fixture!
(Troilus and Cressida
Act I Scene 3)

Timon:
Thus much of this will make
<u>Black white</u>, <u>foul fair</u>, <u>wrong right</u>,
<u>Base noble</u>, <u>old young</u>, <u>coward valiant</u>.
Ha! You gods! why this? What this, you
gods? Why this
Will lug your priests and servants from your
sides,
Pluck stout men's pillows from below their
head:

This yellow slave
Will knit and break religions, bless the accurs'd
Make the hoar leprosy ador'd; place thieves,
And give them title, knee and approbation,
With senators on the bench; this is it
That makes the wappen'd widow wed again...
(Timon of Athens Act IV Scene 3)

Scroop:
White-beards have arm'd their thin and hairless scalps
Against thy majesty. Boys with women's voices
Strive to think big, and clap their female joints
In still unwieldy arms against thy crown.
The very beadsmen learn to bend their bows
Of double-fatal yew against thy state.
Yea, distaff-women manage rusty bills
Against thy seat. Buth young and old rebel,
And all goes worse than I have power to tell.
(Richard II Act III Scene 2)

Synchoresis: [sin kor E sis; Greek, concession, from *synchorein*, to come together, meet]

The rhetorical technique of appearing to agree with those who are against you or disagree with you. The opening of Mark Antony's speech over the body of Caesar is perhaps the most well known example of **synchoresis** as he elaborately pretends to agree with Brutus while subtly changing the crowd's attitude as he continues his speech. This figure often is used by villains such as Richard III and Iago to further their evil plans.

Mark Antony:
Friends, Romans, countrymen, lend me your ears;
I come to bury Caesar, not to praise him;
The evil that men do lives after them,
The good is oft interred with their bones,
So let it be with Caesar. <u>The noble Brutus</u>
<u>Hath told you Caesar was ambitious</u>:
If it were so, it was a grievous fault
And grievously hath Ceacar answered it. . . .
<u>Here, under leave of Brutus and the rest,</u>
<u>(For Brutus is an honorable man</u>
<u>So are they all, all honorable men</u>)
Come I to speak in Caesar's funeral. . .
(Julius Caesar
Act III Scene 2)

Gloucester: [to Lady Ann whom he is wooing by pretending to love her and regretting his former actions]

Vouchsafe to wear this ring.

Anne:
To take is not to give.

Gloucester:
Look how my ring encompasseth thy finger.
<u>Even so thy breast encloseth my poor heart;</u>
Wear both of them, for both of them are thine.
And if <u>thy poor devoted servant</u> may
But bet one favor at thy gracious hand,
Thou dost confirm his happiness forever.

Anne:
What is it?

Gloucester:
That it may please you leave these sad designs
<u>To him that hath most cause to be a mourner,</u>
And presently repair to Crosby House;
Where, <u>after I have solemnly interred</u>
<u>At Chertsey monast'ry this noble king,</u>
<u>And wet his grave with my repentant tears,</u>
<u>I will with all expedient duty see you</u>:
For divers unknown reasons, I beseech you,
Grant me this boon.
Richard III
Act I Scene 2)

Othello:
Give me a living reason she's disloyal.

Iago:
I do not like the office;
But sith I am entered in this cause so far,
<u>Pricked to't by foolish honesty and love,</u>
I will go on. I lay with Cassio lately,
And being troubled with a raging tooth,
I could not sleep.
There are a kind of men so loose of soul,
That in their sleeps will mutter their affairs:
One of this kind is Cassio.
In sleep I heard him say 'Sweet Desdemona,
Let us be wary, let us hide our loves';
And then, sir, would he gripe and wring my hand
Cry 'O sweet creature!' and then kiss me hard,
As if he plucked up kisses by the roots,
That grew upon my lips; then laid his leg
Over my thigh, and sighed, and kissed, and then

Cried 'Cursed fate that gave thee to the Moor!' . . .

Witness you ever-burning lights above,
You elements that clip us round about,
Witness that here Iago doth give up
The execution of his wit, hands, heart,
To wronged Othello's service! Let him command,
And to obey shall be without remorse,
What bloody business ever.
(Othello Act III Scene 3)

Syncope: **[SYN kop e; Greek, *syncope*, a cutting short, from *syn*, together, and *koplein*, to cut]**

Contracting a word by leaving out one of its sounds: ta'en for taken, ne'er for never, o'er for over, e'en for even, i' for in. These examples show how constantly Shakespeare used this technique. See **Hypermonolsyllable** and **Apocope.**

Katharina:
Well ta'en and like a buzzard.
(The Taming of the Shrew Act II Scene 1)

Lust is perjured, murd'rous, bloody, full of blame.
(Sonnet #129)

Agamemnon:
Speak, Prince of Ithaca: and be't of less expect
That matter needless, of importless burden,
Divide thy lips than we are confident,

When rank Thersites <u>opes</u> his mastic jaws,
We shall hear music, wit, and oracle.
(Troilus and Cressida
Act I Scene 3)

Synecdoche: [sy NEK do ke; Greek, *synecdoche,* from *syn,* together and *ekdechsthai*, to receive]

(Puttenham's term: 'the figure of Quick Conceit)

Understanding the whole by one part of it.
A figure of speech by which a more inclusive term is used for a less inclusive term or vice versa, as in 'head' for cattle or 'the law' for police officer. **Puttenham** calls it an allegorical figure and points out its humorous uses, as in the example from *The Merry Wives of Windsor* below:

Mistress Page:
Nay. . .It makes me almost ready to wrangle with mine own honesty: I'll entertain myself like one that I am not acquainted withal; for, sure, unless he know some strain in me, that I know not myself, <u>he would never have boarded me</u> in this fury.

[comparing herself to a ship]

Mistress Ford:
'Boarding' call you it? <u>I'll be sure to keep him above deck</u>.

[keep him above her skirts]

Mistress Page:
So will I: <u>if he come under my hatches, I'll never to sea again</u>

[if he were to come below the doors to the under-decking].

(The Merry Wives of Windsor Act II Scene 1)

Macbeth:
Take thy face [meaning the whole person] hence.

(Macbeth Act V, Scene 3)

Montjoy:
England [meaning the king] shall repent his folly, see his weakness, and admire our sufferance. Bid him therefore consider of his ransom. . .

(Henry V Act III Scene 6)

Cassius:
Rome, [meaning all its citizens] thou hast lost the breed of noble bloods.

(Julius Caesar Act I Scene 2)

Nestor:
Let this be granted, and Achilles' horse
[meaning Achilles' soldiers]
Makes many Thetis' sons.

(Troilus and Cressida Act I Scene 3)

Systrophe: **[SYS tro fe; Greek, collection]**

The piling up of descriptions of something without a final definition. Similar to **synonymia;** also called conglobatio. Shakespeare had an extraordinary energy and imagination for this kind of figure.

Margaret:
Thou elvish-marked, abortive rooting hog,
Thou that was sealed in thy nativity
The slave of nature, and the son of hell:
Thou slander of thy heavy mother's womb,
Thou loathed issue of thy father's loins,
Thou rag of honour!
(Richard III
Act I Scene 3)

Shakespeare's linguistic genius explodes in an outpouring of **systrophe** as Kent vents his anger against the hapless Oswald in *King Lear,* while Mrs. Page finds three ways to describe Sir John Falstaff who has written her an impertinent love letter, and Rosalind finds innumerable ways to describe women's behavior to love-struck men.

Kent:
A knave, a rascal, an eater of broken meats; a base, proud, shallow, beggarly, three-suited, hundred-pound, filthy worsted-stocking knave; a lily-livered, action-taking, whoreson, glass-gazing, super-serviceable, finical rogue; one-trunk-inheriting slave; one that wouldst be a bawd in way of good service, and art nothing but the composition of a knave, beggar, coward, pandar, and the son and heir of a mongrel bitch: one whom I will beat into clamorous whining if thou deni'st the least syllable of thy addition.
(King Lear
Act II Scene 1)

Mistress Page:
What a Herod of Jewry is this! O wicked, wicked world! One that is well-nigh worn to pieces with age to show himself a young gallant! What an unweighed behaviour hath this Flemish drunkard picked (with the devil's name) out of my conversation that he dares in this manner assail me?
(The Merry Wives of Windsor Act II Scene 1)

Rosalind:
He was to imagine me his love, his mistress; and I set him every day to woo me: at which time would I, being but a moonish youth, grieve, be effeminate, changeable, longing and liking, proud, fantastical, apish, shallow, inconstant, full of tears, full of smiles: for every passion something, and for no passion truly anything as boys and women are for the most part cattle of this colour: would now like him, now loath him, then entertain him, then forswear him; now weep for him, then spit at him; that I drave my suitor from his mad humour of love to a living humour of madness.
(As You Like It Act III Scene 2)

Tapinosis: **[ta pi NO sis; Greek, reduction, humiliation, lowness of style]**

Undiginified language that debases a person or thing. (Lanham) when "the dignity or majestie of a high matter is much defaced by the baseness of a word, as to call . . . the Thames a brooke . . .

great wisedome prittie witte." (Peacham) as quoted by Sister Miriam Joseph, (SUAL, p301)

Pandar:
Achilles? A drayman, a porter, a very camel!
(Troilus and Cressida
Act I Scene 2)

Holofernes: [to Moth]
Quis, quis, thou consonant?
(Love's Labour's Lost
Act V Scene 1)

Orsino:
O thou dissembling cub! What wilt thou be
When time hath sow'd a grizzle on thy case?
(Twelfth Night
Act V Scene 1)

Tautologia: [tau to LO gi a; Greek, *tauto*, the same, and *logia*, of words] same as Homiologia.

The vain repetition of the same. Also overuse of alliteration; using too many rhyming endings. Tedious and inane repetition. Justice Shallow Falstaff, Mistress Quickly, Pandar, Fluellen, Nym are all characters whose language is filled with **tautologia.**

See **Homiologia** above for examples.

Topographia: [top o GRA fi a; Greek, *topos*, a place, and *graphia*, writing]

Description of a place.
Sister Miriam Joseph says (SUAL, p321): "The

names of the species of counterfeit representation both factual and fictitious exemplify an unflagging zeal for making distinctions which seem to us mere hair-splitting or wearisome pedantry but which men of the Renaissance evidently found interesting and delightful. In *The Lawiers Logike* Fraunce mentions, with a hint of mild amusement, the species which some of the rhetoricians distinguished. 'If any person be described, they call it *Prosopographia*, if a place, *Topographia*, if a nation, *Chorographia*, if the earth, *Geographia,* If the water, *Hydrographia*, if the wind, *Anemographia*, if a tree, *Dendographia*, if the time *Chronographia,* &c. (vol. 63 v)'."

Shakespeare satirizes this careful, minute characterization of things in Touchstone's declension of the seven causes of a quarrel, in *As You Like It Act V Scene 4*. Quoted in **Aparethmesis** above.

Note that in figures of any length other figures of speech inevitably enter in: **sinonimia, metaphora, assonance, consonance, personification,** and others.

A favorite Shakesperean use of **topographia** is in John of Gaunt's description of the England he knew before the reign of *Richard II.*

Gaunt:
This royal throne of kings, this sceptred isle,
This earth of majesty, this seat of Mars,
This other Eden, demi-paradise,
This fortress built by nature for herself
Against infection and the hand of war,
This happy breed of men, this little world,
This precious stone set in the silver sea,
Which serves it in the office of a wall,
Or as a moat defensive to a house,

Against the envy of less happier lands. . . .
This blessed plot, this earth, this realm, this England. . . .
Dear for her reputation through the world,
Is now leas'd out—I die pronouncing it—
Like to a tenement or pelting farm. . . .
England, bound in with the triumphant sea,
Whose rocky shore beats back the envious siege
Of wat'ry Neptune, is now bound in with shame,
With inky blots, and rotten parchment bonds:
That England, that was wont to conquer others
Hath made a shameful conquest of itself. . .
(King Richard II Act II Scene 1)

Edgar:
Come on, sir, here's the place: stand still; how fearful
And dizzy 'tis to cast one's eyes so low!
The crows and choughs that wing the midway air
Show scarce so gross as beetles. Half way down
Hangs one that gathers samphire—dreadful trade!
Methinks he seems no bigger than his head.
The fishermen that walk upon the beach
Appear like mice: and yond tall anchoring bark
Diminished to her cock; her cock a buoy
Almost too small for sight. The murmuring surge,
That on th'unnumb'red idle pebble chafes,
Cannot be heard so high. I'll look no more,

Lest my brain turn, and the deficient sight
Topple down headlong.
(King Lear
Act IV Scene 6)

Rosalind:
Well, this is the forest of Arden!

Touchstone:
Ay, now am I in Arden, the more fool I. When
I was at home I was in a better place, but
travelers must be content. . . .

Rosalind:
I prithee, shepherd, if that love or gold
Can in this desert place buy entertainment,
Bring us where we may rest ourselves and
feed:
Here's a young maid with travel much
oppressed,
And faints for succor.

Corin:
Fair sir, I pity her. . .
But I am shepherd to another man. . .
Besides his cote, his flocks, and bounds of
feed
Are now on sale, and at our sheepcote now
By reason of his absence there is nothing
That you will feed on. . .

Rosalind:
I pray thee, if it stand with honesty,
Buy thou the cottage, pasture, and the flock,
And thou shalt have to pay of it of us.

Celia:

And we will mend thy wages: I like this place
And willingly could waste my time in it.
(As You Like It
Act II Scene 4)

Tricolon: **[TRI ko lon; Greek, from *tri,* three and *kolon*, limb]**

The division of an idea into three harmonious parts, usually of increasing power. Rhythms of three phrases. See **Isocolon** for a similar but less restrictive figure. This figure gains its power by the ease in which the listening ear picks it up, and the pleasure the listener takes in the powerful rhythm of three. There is a special delight in the complication of the figure in Montjoy's elegant and powerfully phrased threat to Henry V: he repeats the his original figure with additional specifications which constitute the third **tricolon** in a single speech.

Montjoy:
Now we speak upon our cue, and our voice is imperial: England shall repent him his folly, see his weakness, and admire our sufferance. Bid him therefore consider of his ransom; which must proportion the losses we have borne, the subjects we have lost, the disgrace we have digested...For our losses,his exchequer is too poor; for the effusion of our blood, the muster of his kingdom too faint a number; and for our disgrace, his own person, kneeling at our feet, but a weak and worthless satisfaction.
(Henry V
Act III Scene 6)

Richard:

Clifford, ask mercy and obtain no grace.

Edward:
Clifford, repent in bootless penitence.

Warwick:
Clifford, devise excuses for thy faults.

George:
While we devise fell tortures for thy faults.
(Henry VI Part 3
Act II Scene 6)

Lady Anne:
Cursed be the hand that made these fatal holes!
Cursed be the heart that had the heart to do it!
Cursed the blood that let this blood from hence!
(Richard III
Act I Scene 2)

Zeugma: **[ZEUG ma; Greek *zeugnynai,* to join]**

(Puttenham's term: 'Single Supply')

A figure of speech in which a verb is applied jointly to multiple nouns. (When the nouns are disparate and the use of the verb carries a different sense with each, the usage is called **syllepsis**, as witness this example: 'We changed our minds and our clothes.' Or this from Alexander Pope: 'Or stain her honor or her new brocade.')

Berowne:
These oaths and laws will prove an idle

scorn—
Sirrah, come on.
(Love's Labour's Lost
Act I Scene 1)

Moth:
The Fox, the Ape, and the Humble-bee
Were still at odds. being bit three.
(Love's Labour's Lost
Act III Scene 1)

Brutus:
the kitchen malkin pins
Her richest lockram 'bout her reechy neck,
Clamb'ring the walls to eye him: stalls, bulks,
windows,
Are smothered up, leads filled and ridges
horsed
In earnestnesss to see him. . .
(Coriolanus
Act II Scene 1)

King Henry:
So minutes, hours, days, months, and years,
Passed over to the end they were created
Would bring white hairs unto a quiet grave.
(Henry VI Part 3
Act II Scene 5)

Conclusion

I conclude with this extensive quotation from Sister Miriam Joseph's *Shakespeare's Use of the Arts of Language* (288-289).

"The formal training which Shakespeare received contributed not only to the breadth and stature of his thought but also to the richness of the gorgeous panoply with which he invested it. His language, fresh, vibrant, exuberant, and free, makes use of the schemes of words as well as the schemes of construction. . . .

With figures of repetition, Shakespeare weaves a haunting harmony of sound; through the schemes of grammar he achieves such control over movement and rhythm that like a figure skater he may dart, poise, turn, plunge, go where he will, his words fraught with penetrating thought and deep feeling – and all this but an art subservient to the larger art of the builder, to plot construction, character creation, and profound insight into human nature and its problems. Yet this myriad-minded man has time for fun and nonsense, for parody and foolery, for mere gleeful bandying of words.

One may read Shakespeare's plays, or see them produced, with attention to any or all these facets of his art. They give pleasure at many levels, as great music does. One who recognizes in the intricate web of harmonic and melodic progressions the chord structures and rhythmic design, and notes the fine gradation and coloring, experiences a deeper and keener delight in music than one who does not perceive these things; he enjoys not only what the untrained listener enjoys but also a detailed intellectual perception of the relation of parts to parts and to the whole.

Similarly, to cultivate the alert attentiveness to patterns of sound and movement and the expert analysis of thought-relations habitual to educated Elizabethans quickens the responsiveness requisite to a full appreciation of Shakespeare's plays."

I have compiled the figures of speech in this book to help modern-day readers perceive the patterns of sound and movement in Shakespeare's language, so as to increase their admiration for and pleasure in his work.

Appendix

Shakespeare's Spoof of Figures of Speech

It cannot be said that using many learned figures of speech guarantees good writing. Shakespeare himself gives us proof to the contrary. In the play of Pyramus and Thisbe as written and performed by Peter Quince and his amateur company at the end of A Midsummer Nightís Dream, Shakespeare systematically spoofs the use of rhetorical language to the delight of his original audience, and us.

Enter QUINCE for the Prologue

Prologue — Prologue

If we offend, it is with our good will. — Amphibologia
That you should think, we come not to offend, — Enjambment
Antithesis
But with good will. To show our simple skill, — Internal Rhyme
That is the true beginning of our end. — Antithesis
Anastrophe
Consider then we come but in despite.
Catachresis
We do not come as minding to contest you, — Etiologia
Our true intent is. All for your delight
Anastrophe
We are not here. That you should here repent you, — Acyron
The actors are at hand and by their show — Couplet
You shall know all that you are like to know.

Enter Pyramus and Thisbe, Wall, Moonshine, and Lion

Gentles, perchance you wonder at this show;	Apostrophe
But wonder on, till truth make all things plain.	Iambic Pentameter Etiologia
This man is Pyramus, if you would know;	Classical allusion, Partitio
This beauteous lady Thisby is certain.	Forced rhyme, Anaphora
This man, with lime and rough-cast, doth present	Descriptio
Wall, that vile Wall which did these lovers sunder;	Epanorthosis
And through Wall's chink, poor souls, they are content	Pragmatographia
To whisper. At the which let no man wonder.	Paradoxon
This man, with lanthorn, dog, and bush of thorn,	Descriptio
Presenteth Moonshine; for, if you will know,	Personification
By moonshine did these lovers think no scorn	Explanation
To meet at Ninus' tomb, there, there to woo.	Repetition
This grisly beast, which Lion hight by name,	Epithet
The trusty Thisby, coming first by night,	Epithet
Did scare away, or rather did affright;	Correctio
And, as she fled, her mantle she did fall,	Anastrophe, Hyperbaton
Which Lion vile with bloody mouth did stain.	Epithet
Anon comes Pyramus, sweet youth and tall,	Epithet
And finds his trusty Thisby's mantle slain:	Catachresis
Whereat, with blade, with bloody blameful blade,	Alliteration
He bravely broach'd is boiling bloody breast;	Vivid Description
And Thisby, tarrying in mulberry shade,	Topographia
His dagger drew, and died. For all the rest,	Alliteration, Anastrophe
Let Lion, Moonshine, Wall, and lovers twain	Enumratio, Asyndeton
At large discourse, while here they do remain.	Rhymed Couplet

Exeunt Prologue, Thisbe, Lion, and Moonshine.

Enter Pyramus

Pyramus

O grim-look'd night! O night with hue so black! Ploce
O night, which ever art when day is not! Apostrophe, Pleonasmus, Ecphonisis
O night, O night! alack, alack, alack, Epizeuxis
I fear my Thisby's promise is forgot! Anaphora
And thou, O wall, O sweet, O lovely wall, Apostrophe, Epithet, Diacope
That stand'st between her father's ground and mine! Aphaeresis, Descriptio
Thou wall, O wall, O sweet and lovely wall, Apostrophe, Prosopopoei, Pleonasmus, Diacope, Auxesis
Show me thy chink, to blink through with mine eyne! Homiologia

Wall holds up his fingers

Thanks, courteous wall: Jove shield thee well for this! Apostrophe, Epitheton, Classical Allusion
But what see I? No Thisby do I see. Anthypophora, Hyperbaton
O wicked wall, through whom I see no bliss! Apostrophe, Alliteration, Insultatio, Tapinosis, Exclamatio
Cursed be thy stones for thus deceiving me! Assonance

Enter Thisbe

Thisbe

O wall, full often hast thou heard my moans, Exclamatio
For parting my fair Pyramus and me! Epithet
My cherry lips have often kiss'd thy stones, Epithet
Thy stones with lime and hair knit up in thee. Anadiplosis

Pyramus
I see a voice: now will I to the chink, Catachresis, Hypallage
To spy an I can hear my Thisby's face. Thisby! Catachresis, Hypallage

Thisbe
My love, thou art my love I think. Epanorthosis

Pyramus
Think what thou wilt, I am thy lover's grace Anadiplosis
And, like Limander, am I trusty still. Paradigma

Thisbe
And I like Helen, till the Fates me kill. Stychomithia

Pyramus
Not Shafalus to Procrus was so true. Paradigma

Thisbe
As Shafalus to Procrus, I to you. Paradigma

Pyramus
O kiss me through the hole of this vile wall! Epithet, Auxesis

Thisbe
I kiss the wall's hole, not your lips at all. Cacemphaton

Pyramus
Wilt thou at Ninny's tomb meet me straightway? Anastrophe

Thisbe
'Tide life, 'tide death, I come without delay. Aphaeresis

Exeunt Pyramus and Thisbe

Wall
Thus have I, Wall, my part discharged so;
And, being done, thus Wall away doth go. Rhymed Couplet

Exit

Enter Lion and Moonshine

Lion

You, ladies, you, whose gentle hearts do fear	Apostrophe, Paradiastole
The smallest monstrous mouse that creeps on floor,	Alliteration
May now perchance both quake and tremble here,	
When lion rough in wildest rage doth roar.	Epithets
Then know that I, one Snug the joiner, am	Hyperbaton
A lion-fell, nor else no lion's dam;	Catachresis
For, if I should as lion come in strife	Enjambment
Into this place, 'twere pity on my life.	Aphaeresis

Enter Thisbe

Thisbe

This is old Ninny's tomb. Where is my love?	Topographia, Rhetorical Question

Lion

[Roaring] Ohó

Thisbe runs off

The Lion shakes Thisbe's mantle, and exit

Enter Pyramus

Pyramus

Sweet Moon, I thank thee for thy sunny beams;	Apostrophe
I thank thee, Moon, for shining now so bright;	Chronographia
For, by thy gracious, golden, glittering gleams,	Alliteration, Synonyms
I trust to taste of truest Thisby sight.	Alliteration, Hypallage
But stay, O spite!	Rhythm changes to heptameters

But mark, poor knight,	(fourteeners), Anaphora
What dreadful dole is here!	Alliteration
Eyes, do you see?	Anthypophora
How can it be?	Rhetorical question
O dainty duck! O dear!	Alliteration, Apostrophe, Exclamatio, Auxesis, Ecphonisis
Thy mantle good,	Eulogia
What, stain'd with blood!	False rhyme, Descriptio
Approach, ye Furies fell!	Apostrophe
O Fates, come, come,	Repetiton
Cut thread and thrum;	Alliteration
Quail, crush, conclude, and quell!	Synonyms, Cacozelia, Auxesis
O wherefore, Nature, didst thou lions frame?	Rhetorical Question
Since lion vile hath here deflower'd my dear:	Epithet, Encomium
Which is--no, no--which was the fairest dame	Anocoluthon, Aposiopesis, Epanorthosis
That lived, that loved, that liked, that look'd with cheer.	Isocolon Polysyndeton, Enumeratio, Auxesis
Come, tears, confound;	
Out, sword, and wound	
The pap of Pyramus;	
Ay, that left pap,	Epanorthosis
Where heart doth hop:	Descriptio
Stabs himself	
Thus die I, thus, thus, thus.	Epizeuxis

Now am I dead,	Isocolon
Now am I fled;	Anaphora
My soul is in the sky:	Alliteration
Tongue, lose thy light;	Apostrophe
	Catachresis, Hypallage
Moon take thy flight:	Apostrophe, Personification
Exit Moonshine	
Now die, die, die, die, die.	Epizeuxis
Dies	
Re-enter Thisbe	
Thisbe	
Asleep, my love?	Fourteener
What, dead, my dove?	Isocolon
O Pyramus, arise!	Ecphonisis
Speak, speak. Quite dumb?	Isocolon
Dead, dead? A tomb	Anthypophora, Eulogia
Must cover thy sweet eyes.	Encomium, Merismus
These lily lips,	Alliteration, Prosopographia, Partitio
This cherry nose,	Epitheton
These yellow cowslip cheeks,	Descriptio
Are gone, are gone:	Epizeusis
Lovers, make moan:	Apostrophe, Exuscitatio, Hypotyposis
His eyes were green as leeks.	Descriptio
O Sisters Three,	Apostrophe
Come, come to me,	
With hands as pale as milk;	Descriptio
Lay them in gore,	Noema
Since you have shore	Metalepsis

With shears his thread of silk.
Tongue, not a word: Apostrophe

Come, trusty sword; Anaphora
Come, blade, my breast imbrue: Hypallage
Stabs herself

And, farewell, friends;
Thus Thisby ends:
Adieu, adieu, adieu. Epizeuxis
Dies

Theseus
Moonshine and Lion are left to bury the dead.

Demetrius
Ay, and Wall too.

Bottom
[Starting up] No assure you; the wall is down that parted their fathers. Will it please you to see the epilogue, or to hear a Bergomask dance between two of our company? Catachresis Acryon

Selected Bibliography

Ascham, Roger. *The Schoolmaster.* R. J. Schoeck, Ed. Don Mills, Ontario. J.M. Dent & Sons. 1966.

Bate, Jonathan. "The Mirror of Life How Shakespeare Conquered the World." Harper's, April. 2007. pp. 37-46.

Brinsley, John. *Pueriles Confabulatiunculae* 1617. Menston, England: The Scholar Press, 1971.

Culman, Leonardum. *Sententiae Pueriles*. London: Excudebat Eliz. P. 1639.

Elton, Charles Isaac. *William Shakespeare His Family and Friends,* Whitefish, Mt: Kessinger Publishing, 2003.

Greenblatt, Stephen. *Will in the World.* New York, W.W. Norton, 2004.

Harmon, William and C. Hugh Holman. *A Handbook to Literature,* Upper Saddle Roiver, N.J.: Prentice Hill, 2008.

Joseph, Sister Miriam, C.S.C. *Shakespeare's Use of the Arts of Language*. Philadelphia: Paul Dry Books, 2005 (originallycopyrighted 1947).
______*The Trivium*. Philadelphia: Paul Dry Books, 2002 (originallycopyrighted 1937).

Lanham, Richard A. *A Handlist of Rhetorical Terms*. Berkeley: University of California Press, 1969.

Lass, Abraham H, David Kiremidgian and Ruth M. Goldstein. *The*

Wordsworth Dictionary of Classical and Literary Allusion. Ware, Hertfordshire: Wordsworth Reference, 1994.

Lily, William. *A Short Introduction of Grammar Generallie to be Used.* Rebound by Robt. Lunow, MDLVII (1557)

Maguire, Laurie. *Where There's a Will There's a Way* . London: A Perigee Book, Penguin, 2006.

Mulcaster, Richard. *The First Part of the Elementerie which Entreateth Chefelie of the Right writing of our English tung.* London: Thomas Vautroullier, 1582.

O'Dell, Leslie. *Shakespearean Language, A Guide for Actors and Students*. Westport, Connecticut: Greenwood Press, 2002.

Oxford English Dictionary, Second Edition. USA: Oxford University Press, 1989.

Palfrey, Simon and Tiffany Stern. *Shakespeare in Parts.* Oxford: University Press, 2008

Partridge, Eric. *Shakespeare's Bawdy*. London: Routledge and Kegan , 1968.

Riggs, David. *The World of Christopher Marlowe.* New York, Henry Holt and Company, 2004.

Rowse, A.L.. *William Shakespeare, A Biography.* New York: Harper and Row, 1963.

Shapiro, James *1599 A Year in the Life of William Shakespeare*. London: Faber and Faber, 2005

Sherry, Richard. *A Treatise of Schemes and Tropes*. London: John Day, MDL (1550).

______*A Treatise of the Figures of Grammer and Rhetorike*. London: Totill, MDLV (1555).

Smith, John, Gent. *The Mysterie of Rhetorique Unveil'd*. London: E. Coptes for George Eversden, 1665.

Susenbrotum, Joannen. *Epibrammatum Libri II*. Nicol. Brillingerum, 1543.

Vendler, Helen. *The Art of Shakespeare's Sonnets*. Cambridge: The Belknap Press of Harvard University Press, 1997.

Wright, George T. *Shakespeare's Metrical Art.* Berkeley, University of California Press, 1988.

Webster's New Twentieth Century Dictionary of the English Language Unabridged Second Edition. Chicago: The John A. Hertel Company, 1961.

Wood, Clement, Ec. *The Complete Rhyming Dictionary and Poet'sCraft Book*. Garden City, New York: Doubleday and Company, 1936.

Glossary

Figures of Speech in Division by Types (adapted from Richard A. Lanham)

Addition, Subtraction, and Substitution of Letters, Syllables, Words, Phrases and Clauses:

aphaeresis: leaving out a syllable at the beginning of a word
apocope: leave off the last syllable of a word
asyndeton: leaving out conjunctions between words and phrases
diacope: separating parts of a compound word with another word or words
ellipsis: omitting a word understood to be there
paragoge: adding a letter or sound to the end of a word
syncope: leaving out letters or syllables from the center of a word
zeugma: use of one verb to apply to several nouns

Amplifications:

bomphiologia: bombastic speech
diaeresis: dividing genus into several species to amplify
enumeratio: enumerating for emphasis
epitheton: qualifying a noun by adding a descriptive attribution
parenthesis: a thought inserted into a speech as an aside
synonimia: amplification by synonyms
synonym: words with equivalent meaning
systrophe: heaping up descriptions

Argumentative techniques

anacoenosis: asking an opinion from one's listeners or readers
analogy: adducing a parallel case
antanagoge: balancing the favorable side of a case with the unfavorable
anthypophora: asking a question, then answering it
aporia: expressing doubt (real or feigned) about an issue
aposiopesis: breaking off mid-thought

correctio: changing by correcting a previous word or statement
diaerisis: dividing a whole into parts in order to amplify
periphrasis: circumlocution
prolepsis: applying an attribute that will be relevant later

Balance, Antithesis, and Paradox:

antanagoge: balancing the favorable and unfavorable sides of an argument
anthyporphora: asking questions and answering them
antimetabole: inverting the order of words in a phrase
antisagoge: promising a reward for virtue, punishment for lack thereof
antithesis: setting one word or phrase against its opposite
antitheton: same as antitheton
chiasmus: same as antimetabole, inverting the order of words in a phrase
climax: building to an emotional peak through word of increasing weight
enigma: a puzzle or riddle
hypoxeusis: each clause in a compound sentence has both subject and verb
iscolon: repetition of phrases of equal length and identical structure
litotes: a denial of the contrary
oxymoron: words that contradict posited as reality; a condensed paradox
paradox: holding opposites to both be true
polysyndeton: using a conjunction between every clause

Brevity:

brachylogia: to procede by single words
diazeugma: one subject holding for many verbw
oxymoron: a paradox condensed to two words
zeugma: use of a single word to govern several subsequent words or clauses

Description:

descriptio: describing a person, place or thing
chronographia: describing the time of day or seasons
hypotyposis: describing actions
onomotopoeia: using words that sound like the thing they express

pragmatographia: heightened description of an event or an action
prosopographia: description of imaginary entitities or persons
topographia: description of imaginary, nonexistent places

Emotional Appeals:

anacoenosis: asking one's listeners their opinion
aporia: expressing doubt (true or feigned) about an issue
apostrophe: stopping discourse to address a present or absent person or thing
ecphonesis: an exclamation to express emotion
encomium: a speech praising a person
eulogia: calling a blessing on a person, place, or thing
exuscitatio: stirring up hearers to feelings like those of the speaker
inter se pugnantia: pointing out the difference between theory and practice
orcos: an oath
sarcasmus: a bitter taunt
tapinosis: language debasing a person or thing

Metaphorical Substitutions and Puns

allegory: a lengthened comparison or metaphor
analogy: comparison by finding a parallel circumstance
antanaclasis: a pun involving a homonym
antonomasia: substituting a proper name for the idea it represents
asteismus: picking up a word and playing on it mockingly
cacemphaton: lewd image, scurrilous jest
catachresis: farfetched, extravagant metaphor
hyperbole: exaggerated, extravagant description
irony: saying the opposite of what is meant
meiosis: using language to belittle, often focusing on a single word
metalepsis: attributing a present situation to a remote cause
metonymy: substituting an attribute or feature for the whole
paronomasia: making puns; playing on the sounds of words
personification: turning non-human elements into human beings
simile: saying something is like something else, .
synecdoche: substitution of a part for the whole or vice versa

Repetition of clauses and phrases:

auxesis: words or phrases arranged in climactic order

commoratio: repeating a strong point several times for emphasis
epimone: a refrain; frequent repetition of a phrase
epistrophe: repeating the same word at the end of a series of phrases
homiologia: tedious, redundant style of speech
isocolon: repetition of phrases of equal length and similar structure
plonasmus: needless repetition of what is already understoon
tautologia: repetition of the same idea in different words.

Repetition of sounds:

alliteration: using the same consonant sound at the beginning of a series of word
assonance: resemblance of neighboring sounds
parimion: each word in a sentence begins with the same sound

Repetition of words:

anadiplosis: using the last word of a clause or sentence to begin the next
anaphora: repetition of the same word to begin a series of clauses or sentences
antistasis: repetition of a word but in a contrary or changed sense
antistrope: repetition of a word at the end of several successive clauses or sentences
auxesis: words or phrases arranged in climactic order
diacope: repetition of a word with words inbetween
epanalepsis: repeating the initial word of a sentence at the end
epistrophe: repeating the closing word at the end of several clauses or sentences
epizeuxis: rerpetition of a word with no words in between
homoioteleuton: like endings; a series of words ending alike
hypoxeusis: every clause in a sentence has its own subject and verb
ploce: repetition of a word with new meaning after the intervention of another word
polyptoton: repetition of words from the same root but with different endings
polysyndeton: use of many conjunctions
symploce: a series of clauses beginning and ending with the same words

Ungrammatical or Unusual Uses of Language:

amphibologia: confusing grammatical structure, often from poor punctution

anacoluthon: changing structure mid sentence

anastrophe: unusual word order in clauses or sentences

anthimeria: using one part of speech for another

antiphrasis: irony expressed in one word

barbarismus: mispronunciations or a word used wrong

cacozelia: affected diction especially using unnecessary Latin words

catachresis: miss-use of words, malapropisms

enallage: substitution of one part or kind of speech for another

hendyadis: using two nouns connected by 'and' instead of a noun and adjective

hypallage: words used in an unexpected and illogical way

hyperbaton: a departure from the normal word order

hysteron proteron: words out of order where the one that normally goes first goes last

malapropism: using words that sound alike for the wrong meaning

noema: overly subtle or obscure speech

solecismus: ignorant misuse of cases, genders, and tenses of words

soriasmus: mixing of languages ignorantly

syllepsis: one verb lacking congruence with one of the subject it governs

Index